Praise for *The Really (*

'The need for this book has never bee_____
in increasingly dynamic environment._____ to be able to
iterate quickly, assimilate opinions and data, evaluate options and
decide where to invest your effort. This same challenge is experienced by individuals, entrepreneurs, product managers to people
that run mature businesses. Julia manages to synthesise this difficult problem into a simple process for evaluating and acting upon
your really good idea!'

**Alastair Moore, Senior Teaching Fellow,
UCL School of Management**

'Refreshingly straightforward way to put the customer at the heart
of everything you do.'

Camilla Tress, Innovation Lead, Oliver Bonas

'Before new ideas get any investment, they should be put to this test.'

**Ian Merricks, Managing Partner at White Horse Capital,
Chair at The Accelerator Network**

'An essential DIY toolkit for improving your offering.'

Lauren Bigelow, Chief Product Officer, IMVU

'Coming up with ideas isn't the hard part, knowing which to take
forward is. *The Really Good Idea Test* is full of valuable insight and
practical tips, testament to Julia's rich experience.'

**Marc Abraham, Head of Product at ASOS,
formerly Notonthehighstreet & World First**

'Thank you for writing this book! I will be sharing it with my teams so that they build on validated ideas rather than fulfil requirements with no evidence of need or value.'

Mel Lang, Agile Coach at Alpha Health,
formerly at Xing, Nokia, FT & Gamesys

'Much more than a test, Julia's book takes the reader through a compendium of modern product management thinking and it should be required reading for anyone building new products and services.'

Daniel Appelquist, Director of Advocacy
for Samsung Internet

'This test gives us fresh perspectives and clarity to make tricky decisions.'

Caroline Wheeler, Market Research Consultant

'Don't waste 6 months working on your idea to find out it won't work. Read this book and save yourself a lot of grief!'

Colin Hayhurst, Serial Entrepreneur, CEO of Mojeek,
(sold businesses to TripAdvisor & ANSYS)

'There is no idea whose chances of success wouldn't get a massive boost from these fiercely practical insights and ready-to-use tools. This is one test we'll keep on taking.'

Richard Stagg, Director, Product Management, Pearson

'We encourage our scientists and researchers to use these 7 steps as soon as a commercial idea crops up.'

Professor Sean Ryan, Exec. Director,
South-East Physics Network

The Really Good Idea Test

Pearson

At Pearson, we have a simple mission: to help people make more of their lives through learning.

We combine innovative learning technology with trusted content and educational expertise to provide engaging and effective learning experiences that serve people wherever and whenever they are learning.

From classroom to boardroom, our curriculum materials, digital learning tools and testing programmes help to educate millions of people worldwide – more than any other private enterprise.

Every day our work helps learning flourish, and wherever learning flourishes, so do people.

To learn more, please visit us at **www.pearson.com/uk**

The Really Good Idea Test

Get Evidence. Make Decisions.
Move Forward.

Julia Shalet

Pearson

Harlow, England • London • New York • Boston • San Francisco • Toronto • Sydney • Dubai • Singapore • Hong Kong
Tokyo • Seoul • Taipei • New Delhi • Cape Town • São Paulo • Mexico City • Madrid • Amsterdam • Munich • Paris • Milan

PEARSON EDUCATION LIMITED

KAO Two
KAO Park
Harlow CM17 9SR
United Kingdom
Tel: +44 (0)1279 623623
Web: www.pearson.com/uk

First edition published 2020 (print and electronic)

ISBN: 978-1-292-32709-9 (print)
       978-1-292-32710-5 (PDF)
       978-1-292-32711-2 (ePub)

British Library Cataloguing-in-Publication Data
A catalogue record for the print edition is available from the British Library

Library of Congress Cataloging-in-Publication Data
A catalog record for the print edition is available from the Library of Congress

10 9 8 7 6 5 4 3 2 1
24 23 22 21 20

Cover design by Two Associates

Print edition typeset in Charter ITC Pro 10/14 by SPi Gobal
Printed by Ashford Colour Press Ltd, Gosport

NOTE THAT ANY PAGE CROSS REFERENCES REFER TO THE PRINT EDITION

Contents

Publisher's acknowledgements

___

4, 7, 9, 11, 58, 60, 77, 78, 79, 100, 102, 103, 137, 139, 152, 155, 180, 181, 182, 198, 199, 200 **Nic Hinton:** Nic Hinton; **35 The Nielsen Company (US), LLC:** Three Common Causes of Innovation Failure, The Nielsen Company (US), LLC, 24-05-2018.

GETTING STARTED

THE
REALLY
GOOD IDEA
TEST

KEY POINTS

Discover how The Really Good Idea Test can work for you

Get an introduction to the seven steps of the test

Adopt the ground rules to get the most you can out of this test

What is The Really Good Idea Test?

The Really Good Idea Test ® will help you find out if your idea is worth pursuing. The test takes you on a practical seven-step journey. It starts with writing a hypothesis where you will find a new way to articulate your idea, making it clear who you intend to create benefit for and what you are trying to achieve overall. As you move through the steps you will identify where you need to gather extra evidence as you identify your riskiest assumptions. Next you will design, carry out and analyse your own research so that by the end of the test you will have enough evidence to make a decision whether to pursue your idea or not. That decision can be made with confidence as it is based on evidence you have gathered, not on your gut feel or best guess.

With common pitfalls to avoid and top tips signalled throughout, this test is hands-on and will get into the nitty gritty of why, when, what, how and where to carry out research to get evidence required to make an informed decision. You will see how to write smart research questions and carry out interviews that are designed to uncover the truth about how people really feel, think and behave.

This test is an early checkpoint to see if you have a good idea or not. It is the first place to go when you have an idea and it is a test you can return to whenever you need to get some confidence to proceed. It will work for you whenever you have a new idea, whether it is for a new or existing product or service. The test will help you to avoid falling into the trap of spending time, money and effort developing a proposition, solution and brand, only then to find out that it is not what the customer wants or needs.

The best thing about this test is that you can do it on your own, as soon as you have an idea, without relying on anyone else. This is an early-stage test to find out if your idea is as good as you think it might be. You can carry it out in stealth-mode before you talk to any colleagues or collaborators about it. It is not a fully blown large-scale piece of market research that can cost thousands. It is a self-contained piece of early investigation so that you can say with confidence that you have a really good idea.

You could be through this whole process in just a few weeks. You could complete Steps 1 to 5 in a matter of days, sitting at your desk. Recruiting interviewees could take around a week, with another week to carry out research and three days analysing the results so you can make your decisions. Of course, you can choose to go at your own pace – everyone is different.

I have crafted The Really Good Idea Test through twenty plus years of working with new propositions and products, features and services as a product owner, project director, qualitative researcher and a product coach, helping innovators to do it for themselves. I will share examples from my experiences across many sectors and environments to explain why I say what I do, from working in and with start-ups, small and medium enterprises, corporates and the third sector. Within the seven steps I will share tools I have developed, along with best practice from well-established and modern approaches that I have tried and tested myself.

Who is The Really Good Idea Test for?

You have an idea. It could be a proposition, product, service, feature, marketing plan, project or business and you think it could be a *really good idea*. Your idea might be for a brand-new venture or it might be to do with an existing product or service. For example, you want to take your existing product to another market or customer segment that you think may behave differently to your existing market.

This test is for you if:

- You are spending a lot of time mulling your idea over and you want help to get off the starting block.
- You have ideas but you never seem to do anything with them.
- You know that so many new ideas fail and you want to give yours the best chance of success.
- You have the pressure to stay ahead of the game and want to understand whether modern approaches will help you to move faster.
- You have lots of experience working with new ideas and want to try a different way to quickly validate them.
- You have no experience developing new ideas and you do not appreciate business jargon.
- You are working on an initiative on your own, or for a small, medium or massive organisation.

From now on, I am going to refer to you, and all those people I have worked with who have ideas, as 'innovators'. You may not see yourself as an innovator, but the word comes from the Latin *innovare,* which means renew, and is based on the root *novus,* which means new. So whether you are working on an idea that is improving something or doing something totally new, you are to me and for the purposes of this book, an innovator!

How this test works

Seven practical steps

There are seven steps in The Really Good Idea Test which must be taken in chronological order.

As you progress through each step, you will find yourself wanting to make changes, to iterate and improve upon what you have done in previous steps. This going backwards is indicated in the diagram by the dotted lines. Iterating is fundamentally positive behaviour as it gives you the flexibility to be able to go back and make improvements at any time. You must, however, work through the seven steps chronologically. So if, for example, you are at Step 5 (Measures and targets) and you realise that you need to make a change in Step 1 (Write hypothesis), then you must go right back and work through Step 2 (Identify risks), Step 3 (Create questions), Step 4 (Find interviewees) until you arrive at the point you were in Step 5 (Measures and targets).

Templates for those working on an idea right now

You can engage with this book without using this series of templates, but for those of you who are wanting to spring into action as you read, it will help you get up and running right now.

Research-ready templates

The templates will give you a place to store and share your thoughts and workings as you progress through all seven steps. Using the templates will help you understand the process better and will help you to prepare well before you carry out the interviews. They will also help you to carry out consistent research conversations and push you to document all your results. This will give you a way to not only explain to others what you learnt through The Really Good Idea Test but also ensures that you record everything for when you want to come back and review them at a later stage. You are likely to find some important information in your templates to underpin your future business case assumptions. You can find all the templates at productdoctor.co.uk.

There is a CORE template to use throughout the test. You start filling it out in Step 1 (Write hypothesis) and update it as you take each step of the test. Step 6 (Conduct interviews) and Step 7 (Analyse and decide) both have one-page templates that complement the CORE.

Step 6 has a one-page template that is called CHECKLISTS. The CORE and CHECKLISTS templates together become the full research script to take into every research interview.

The CHECKLISTS template has prompts on how to open and close the interview and places where you need to make notes during the research interview.

Step 7 also has a one-page template that is called RESULTS. This template works as a summary for each group of interviews with spaces to share your decision and rationale. The RESULTS one pager provides a succinct format to see the overall findings across the group of interviews that have been conducted. If you need more detail, then you can of course refer back to your CORE and CHECKLISTS, so these become supporting documents.

To recap, there are three templates that all work together.

1 The CORE template is in play right from the start in Step 1 (Write hypothesis) and stays with you throughout all seven steps. It is taken with you into the interviews in Step 6 as it contains the questions you need to ask and provides the place to scribble down the scores. As you are going to scribble on it in each interview, it also becomes a great record of what happened plus it has crucial information for scoring the results in Step 7.

2 The CHECKLISTS template tops and tails the research interview and so it supports the CORE which has the middle bit – the interview questions and measures to score. This is completed in Step 6.

3 The RESULTS template is for documenting the output of each group of interviews. This will help you to get clarity on the interview analysis and the decision that needs making and is a succinct format to share results with others. This is completed in Step 7.

The CORE stays with you throughout The Really Good Idea Test

1 WRITE HYPOTHESIS

Enter Step 1's Four-Part Hypothesis

4 FIND INTERVIEWEES

Enter Step 4's Recruitment Criteria & Mix for Group Profile

CORE THE REALLY GOOD IDEA TEST	**2 IDENTIFY RISKS**	**3 CREATE QUESTIONS**	**5 MEASURES & TARGETS**	
Section A: Does the problem, need or desire exist?	*Enter Step 2's Risky Assumptions*	*Enter Step 3's Questions*	*Enter Steps 5's Individual Measures*	*Enter Step 5's Group Targets*
Section B: Are the existing solutions good enough to solve their problem/meet their needs or desires?			&	&
Section C: Are they prepared to take the necessary actions to get another solution?			*Write Step 6's Scores*	*Write Step 7's scores*
Section D: (Optional) How do they feel about your idea?			**6 CONDUCT INTERVIEWS**	**7 ANALYSE & DECIDE** STOP

On the CORE template you will see space to write:

- Hypothesis from Step 1 (Write hypothesis)
- Risky assumptions from Step 2 (Identify risks) categorised under four sections (A, B, C and D)
- Interview questions from Step 3 (Create questions) that will get the interviewee to give information to evidence the risky assumptions
- Group profile from Step 4 (Find interviewees) that lists out the recruitment criteria and mix of interviewees
- Measures and targets from Step 5 which, set against the risky assumptions, give a way to score the responses that interviewees give in Step 6 (Conduct interviews)
- Group targets and scores from Step 5 which give a way to measure and analyse the scores across the total group in Step 7 (Analyse and decide)

The RESULTS template is completed in Step 7 (Analyse and decide)

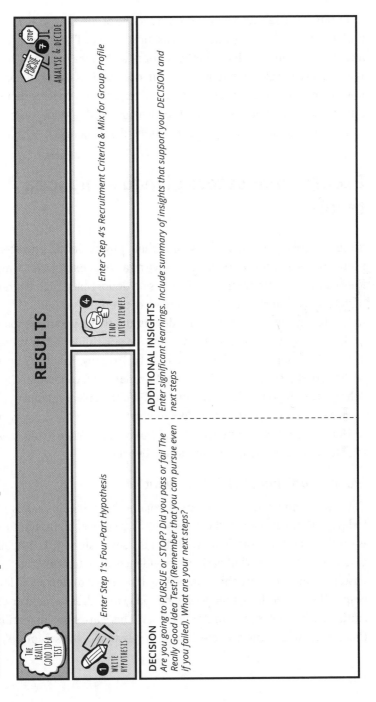

RESULTS

THE REALLY GOOD IDEA TEST

PURSUE · STOP · 7 · ANALYSE & DECIDE

WRITE HYPOTHESIS (1)

Enter Step 1's Four-Part Hypothesis

FIND INTERVIEWEES (4)

Enter Step 4's Recruitment Criteria & Mix for Group Profile

DECISION
Are you going to PURSUE or STOP? Did you pass or fail The Really Good Idea Test? (Remember that you can pursue even if you failed). What are your next steps?

ADDITIONAL INSIGHTS
Enter significant learnings. Include summary of insights that support your DECISION and next steps

In this RESULTS template, you can see the original hypothesis and the profile for the group that was interviewed. There is space to add the decision, which is whether to pursue the idea or stop. There is also space for additional insights which is for all of the rich information that you will discover during the research interviews that is outside of the numeric scores for the measures and targets.

You can find all the templates at productdoctor.co.uk.

Excuses innovators give to avoid idea testing!

It seems bonkers to pursue a vision without any evidence; however, there are some innovators that will give a range of excuses for why they cannot test out their idea! There is no doubt that a high degree of determination is required to get new ideas off the ground. All innovators have stories of ups and downs and thank goodness some of them hung on in there. But how many do you think have a strong enough intuition, coupled with fortune, to drive towards success without first testing out their ideas? How many can you name? Steve Jobs maybe? If you are that one in a million, then please, I don't want to stop you – put this book down now!

Here are some regular excuses that innovators give to avoid testing out their ideas with customers and/or users:

'People don't know what they want'

There are innovators who will argue that nothing like this exists today, so they cannot test their ideas out. I need to explain that there is rarely something totally new. Within the seven steps of The Really Good Idea Test, as part of gathering evidence for potential target customer and/or user behaviour, you will be asked to find some kind of parallel – something that people do today to address a need or fulfil a desire that is in a similar category. There are some inventions that people will argue are totally new; for example, the steam train.

I argue that rather than being something totally new, the steam train was a better (faster and cheaper) way to get from A to B.

In 1810, travelling by horse and cart from London to Bristol would take you a few days. By the 1840s it was possible to do the same journey in a matter of hours, travelling at speeds of around 60 mph on a steam train. So aren't most things just a more convenient, quicker, cheaper and/or more enjoyable way of doing something that people already do?

'But I must use this technology'

The Really Good Idea Test puts people at the heart of innovation, rather than the other way around. That has been my mantra at Product Doctor (productdoctor.co.uk) ever since I set it up. So often innovators start with a capability or a bit of technology and work it out from there. I am not saying that this approach always fails, but in my experience it is not the most efficient way to develop a new idea. It usually requires back-pedalling to find a customer and/or user need and some frustration, especially as money will have been sunk into building solutions that do not yet have a market.

The opposite of putting people at the heart of innovation is that you try to put the innovation at the heart of people. This is where I find myself often saying 'just because you can, doesn't mean you should'.

Here is a story that shows the repercussions of coming from a technology-first position

Story: Shelving a ten-million-pound investment as it did not meet basic usability

I was asked by a new Chief Operations Officer to review a voice recognition platform he had bought from a large supplier. Ignoring the broader strategic intentions, I wanted to test the functionality and see if it worked. The vision was that we would be able to use our voice to navigate through services from our mobile phone, rather than press buttons. Rather than start with business cases (which had naturally been provided by the technology supplier), I wanted to see what the customer experience would be. I found that we had set it up in a test environment and I could try it out for myself. I sat for a few hours, trying out different angles with the engineer, but it just didn't work.

As you will know, voice recognition is now in massive growth. There are a number of scenarios where it works really well, for example as people float around their homes giving various instructions to their smart speakers! Twenty years on and this is how long it took to get it working! The COO had great vision, but it was definitely too early. He taught me an important lesson: he applauded my direct and simple recommendation to 'just stop working on it'. How he hated long PowerPoint presentations! He told me that he did not know many people who would have the guts to deliver this news after he had made the investment. He also applauded the fact that this would save the company from sinking more money into something that was not ready and he asked me where I would redeploy the resources. My work life suddenly got a whole lot more interesting! This is a great advert for getting the confidence to just STOP.

Many innovators start explaining their ideas as a new technology or capability that has just become available and they are keen to find an application for it. I have seen this frequently in those applying for government funding, where there are many competitions themed around a particular technology. Just because you can whizz and bang doesn't mean you should!

I ask that you step back and start thinking about the value you can add for people. If you start properly with Step 1 (Write hypothesis), you will put aside your capabilities (the things you can do) and take a moment to look at the problem / need. This is putting people at the heart of innovation.

'I have already built the product'

So are you prepared to throw good money after bad? Perhaps you have heard of the 'sunk cost fallacy'? It is the behaviour of continuing because you have already invested time, money or effort. It is like the all-you-can-eat restaurant and the negative effects of over-eating to get money's worth! There can be a huge amount of spend required to get a product, service or new experience to market. Once you have factored in the cost to build it, there is testing and making it robust, ensuring compliance with the relevant best practice guidelines and regulations, the customer support arrangements, channel and partner relationships to develop plus branding, PR and all the marketing. Before you invest all that additional spend to get your idea to market are you sure you are delivering something that people want and prepared to pay for? It certainly seems to be human nature to plough straight into finding a solution, and now it is easier than ever to use prototyping tools or even start developing ideas with mainstream available tech tools. But please don't fall into this trap. If you have already gone down the path and started to build an early prototype, stop for the time being, put it to one side and let's wind back – it is not too late!

'I have nothing to show yet'

It is never too early to start talking with potential users and customers. So many innovators I have worked with think that they need to show some kind of prototype or even fully built product in order to get any customer and/or user feedback at all. I argue the opposite, that at this early stage, you have a hypothesis and that is what needs testing, preferably before you have anything to show!

I would advise against showing them anything until you are sure that you have exhausted first the conversation about whether the problem, need or desire exists and how they work around it. When you show people a mock-up or prototype of an idea, you bring them straight into talking about a solution before you know whether they have a problem, desire or need for a solution. People also will find it more difficult to be critical about something that looks as if it is already built or fully visualised.

So the mindset here is to be comfortable in starting conversations with potential users and customers even if you don't have anything to actually show them. This is a good discipline as it stops you going too far in the product design and experience before you confirm that your customer and user segments exist along with their problems, needs and desires.

Here is a story from working with mobile application ('app') developers. As people who can-do, they can be inclined to jump to solutions and are keen to get their product out there before they have found out whether the problem, need or desire exists. If they were to do this research before they started building, they would avoid building a solution for a market that may not exist.

Story: Developers seeking their first piece of customer feedback on a live app

Many developers have told me that they are getting their customer feedback. They have developed an app and put it live on to an app store. This is the first time they have been in contact in any way with any users or customers.

The people who are downloading and trying out the app will mostly give you feedback on how it works – the usability – feedback on their experience. But hang on, you are not testing market fit at this point: Does your solution address an actual need, problem or desire? You are learning about their experience of using the app.

This is the sort of feedback that you will get – taken from some reviews of new apps on the Android store:

'. . . This app is awful. It crashes and it doesn't work constantly. . . '

'. . . The interface is poor, with too many clicks to get to the appropriate screen. . . '

'. . . This app feels like it was drastically rushed to be launched. Bloated, slow and has a lovely new inconsistent design. . . '

It is a particular type of person who will give you feedback on the app store so you are only reaching a group of people who have a personality type that likes to give feedback. They may even be serial critics, watching for the latest thing, giving feedback and then moving on to the next new thing. You may have heard the phrase 'early adopter'. These are people who are inclined towards being one of the early groups to start using new products and services. Well these commenters may well be even earlier than those – they may have no intention of sticking with you so are really not your target audience and a large proportion of these are unlikely to become your revenue generating users.

This type of product testing is a later stage. These developers had no idea whether the people who gave the feedback had downloaded the app because they had a genuine need or desire for it, or whether they are serial downloaders and just people who like to test out new things and give feedback.

Put another way, I have seen innovators spend a lot of time diving into the feasibility, where the question is 'Can we technically do it?' and working on the viability, where the question is 'Can it scale?'. The question they ought to be asking before getting too deeply into those is about desirability, which is the question of 'Is there a user problem, need and/or desire?'. We must start here.

Ground rules

To get the most out of this test and book, there are some things you need to be prepared to do.

Understand the difference between a customer and a user

I refer to 'users' and 'customers'. A user is someone that 'uses' the product or service you are creating; they may be a different person from the 'customer' – who is the one who pays for the use of the product or service. Or they may be the same person. In a business scenario, an IT Director may be the one who has the budget to buy a customer account management system that is going to be used by customer service agents. So, the IT Director is the customer and the customer service agent is the user. What about a family summer holiday to an all-inclusive hotel with a kids' club? The parent is the customer, paying for the holiday and the user is their happy child who will get to enjoy it without a care in the world! This is the reason why, throughout this test, I will refer to customers and/or users. It is a prompt for you to think about the different people involved in making your idea a success and most importantly, if the user and the customer are different to each other, then do not assume that what pleases one will please the other.

Meet your customer and/or user face-to-face

I hope you are now of the opinion that without engaging with your customers and/or users, you are in danger of producing solutions that do not meet market needs and may be built around problems that are not as big or painful as you think. The worst result ever is that your solution is not wanted or needed after you have spent significant time and effort developing it.

Engaging with customers and/or users is a behaviour that you need to continue as you take your idea further into development and beyond the launch. 'Engage' is a very active verb as it is about attracting and keeping someone's interest. Engagement is something that needs to be felt and you cannot do that if you have distance between you and the customer. When I use the word here, I mean actual face-to-face conversation, looking into the eyes of the right people while you interview them.

Story: The moment I realised that I could go and engage with customers myself

One of the first products I managed was voicemail. This was the early days of personal mobile phones and it was for one of the major UK mobile networks. A new product director had just been brought in and asked me what my customers thought of their voicemail experience and I could not answer, after all that was the realm of the research department, wasn't it? As she asked around the product managers in the rest of her new department, she heard the same answer and very quickly had us all trained by a leading innovation agency. This was a turning point for me. We all became product managers who did their own qualitative research, gathering insights and evidence to support new ideas for products, features and marketing plans. By doing this, as a team, we improved our revenues, bringing better initiatives to market more quickly. Change was driven by customer understanding and we no longer needed to fight for market research team resources.

Carry out customer and/or user interviews yourself

I will talk about being able to carry out this research yourself. 'DIY Research' (do it yourself) if you will. If you are working in a larger organisation, it may be that you have access to people who could help you; for example, a sales team, who may be able to run this test directly with potential customers and/or users as they go out into the field. So 'do it yourself' could mean that you can draft in other people who can help you reach your target interviewees and they can carry out the interview for you. Be sure to give them all the same research script to keep all the interviews consistent and I would still do some yourself.

Some people I have trained are very concerned about their ability to DIY and carry out interviews themselves. I do accept that there are some people who struggle to play the role of the neutral researcher as it does not suit all personalities:

a) Some people cannot help but sell. They are unable to put on 'research face'. They are just too enthusiastic, which influences interviewees in research and creates bias in their responses. They will just want to please the interviewer. These enthusiasts are more likely to spend the time talking rather than listening.

b) Some people can be very 'binary'. They see black and white and ignore the grey. The grey areas can contain some very interesting insight. They like to stick to their script very rigidly, with every intention of getting through their questions with no deviation. They are going to miss clues that interviewees give them. They will miss the slight hesitation in the answer, the pauses before responses, the change of tone in the voice. All of these are opportunities for the interviewer to probe further, 'Why did you hesitate then? You paused when you answered that, what were you thinking? Your tone changed then, why was that?'. These are gold dust; opportunities to really understand people's motivations that often lie hidden behind what they actually say.

c) Some people are just not comfortable talking with strangers and for them this would be a painful and entirely unwanted experience!

If you are one of these people that is okay. There is a suggestion in Step 6 (Conduct interviews) of how you can practice your research skills and get someone else to help you identify where you need to improve. If you really think that there is no hope, then you can find someone who can carry out the face-to-face research for you and get them involved. If you are doing interviews in pairs or groups, then you could join the session, but I do not recommend for one-on-one interviews as it can be intimidating for the respondent and honestly, if you feel uncomfortable that will also come across in your body language!

Get used to iterating

You are going to find yourself questioning what you have done in previous steps and wanting to go back and make changes. If you ignore these urges and just carry on, then you are not going to get the most out of the test. If you go back and make changes to a previous step, you also need to follow the discipline of going through all the following steps again in chronological order to get back to where you were. Don't be daunted – it may be that you just need to make small tweaks. Spending a little more time going backwards and forwards now, checking and reviewing what you are doing, could be the difference between success and failure later on.

Pause to make evidence-based decisions

Once you have completed The Really Good Idea Test you will be at a decision point with evidence you can now act upon. Recognising you are at this point and that a decision needs to be made is really important. Instead of forging forward regardless, it will encourage you to look at the evidence you have collected and take stock of your current confidence level to proceed. Get in front of that mirror and look yourself in the eye. It is time for honesty and the question is simple: 'Should I pursue or stop?'.

Don't be afraid to STOP

Being prepared to stop is vital. It's an anti-waste exercise and there is no shame in it. In fact, it is an opportunity to stop throwing good money, time, effort, resources and energy after bad. Remember that even after the cost of building the product itself, significant sums of money can be required to bring a product to market. It costs to create a great customer experience, to set up good customer support and to launch. In 1998 I got the nickname the 'Product Killer' and I am rather proud of it! By stopping, the company was able to re-deploy resources to work on something that was revenue positive. For all ideas at all stages, allow yourself to change tack or stop work altogether. Learn from failures quickly and move on. You have learned loads from this not working out and are now better practised to succeed next time!

Strive to be objective

It would be quite easy to trick yourself through this test. You could pretend that certain questions don't need answering. You could hear only what you want to hear. You could brush difficulties under the carpet. But if you want to really make sure that you do not waste time, effort and money, you will take the advice throughout this test to keep yourself as neutral as you can. Look yourself straight in the eye and be honest with yourself. So please do not ignore that voice in your head or that person on your shoulder asking 'Really?!'.

Spring into action as you read

The best scenario here is that you have an idea to work on and can spring straight into action as you are reading. This is a step-by-step guide written in plain English. You should be able to pick it up and start applying it from the get-go. It is a practical workbook, not a theoretical piece of prose, so slide it into your bag (virtually, if you have the e-book version) and start applying the steps to your own potentially 'really good' idea(s).

Are you working in an organisation or with investors?

The Really Good Idea Test works for people who have ideas, regardless of whether they are working entirely on their own or not.

Naturally, if you are working with investors or in an organisation that has its own processes, you need to be able to explain what you are doing to get support for this approach. Here are some common areas where discussion arises and some tips on how to deal with them.

It's too early for a business case

When you present your idea (pre or post The Really Good Idea Test), perhaps for funding or to get through an approval stage, I guarantee that there will be people who will ask questions that are too advanced. Typically, they may ask about your business case, where you will need to have factored in when you are going to make money / get traction, when you are going to break even, what channels you are going to use to get to market and so on. Please resist being pushed to do a business case at this early stage. It is too early to start going into solution detail and delivery. Many good ideas get stopped by this line of questioning.

You need to be very clear that you cannot possibly work out the answers to these questions until you have established that the problem, need or desire exists in the first place. You can show them the seven steps and your completed CORE template to explain the point further and show your focus on getting evidence for the risky assumptions before you dive too far into solutions. Explain that before you do anything else you need to show confidence in your initial hypothesis, then you will know if it is worth pursuing. You must resist designing solutions before you have evidence of this first principle. This is how you are going to make sure that you do not waste money on building solutions that do not have a customer.

How to make the case for a small amount of funds

Throughout this test, I will give you low-cost options as this test really is something you should be able to do yourself, in your own time and with a low (or maybe no) budget. The majority of any spend is likely to be on paying interviewees to talk honestly with you. If your team has some budget then you may be able to tap into that.

You may have some kind of 'innovation fund' if your organisation has put aside money to experiment with ideas and invest incrementally in testing out ideas. The idea of incremental, smaller investments is that we can learn as we go with less waste along the way. So if we need to stop progressing an idea, that is ok as we have not sunk too much cost into it. The fund is to allow small investments to experiment with new ideas and some are expected to fail. That is life. So, if you have a fund for idea testing, then go for it!

If it needs a budget and no funds are available, then you may like to get your organisation to think of the value of setting some aside. A deal needs to be struck between finance and the product / innovating managers. Here is how you can position it:

Making the case to get budget put aside for idea testing:

We need to set aside a budget of x for research and testing new ideas so we can innovate.

This is not a large-scale market research project. It is light testing of early stage ideas which we can do ourselves, in our own time, and work out which ideas are worth pursuing.

We will use the funds to make sure that there are problems, need and desires for us to address before we jump to building solutions.

We are spending in the smallest increments possible and learning as we go, so we can then work out where to best invest the larger amounts.

We need a fast and efficient way to access those funds. You do not need to be as cautious as you are with the larger investments as we just need small increments to allow us to experiment. So the decision-making process needs to be quick and it can be signed off by someone at a lower level in the organisation.

Explain you are going to do the research yourself

Some organisations will choose to see this as 'research' and think that it should go through the Marketing, Customer Insights and/ or Research Department. This is just one of a number of very early new ideas, hypothetical punts, that you are working on and it would be good to set up a way of working that enables you a clear path to carry out your own testing.

Here are some arguments you can use if this happens:

a) This research is at a VERY early stage. You are at the point where you need to work out if your hunch is worthy of being called an idea and whether that idea is worth progressing. So, you would not want to take up resources of the research department until you know that it is a GOOD idea, right?

b) All companies I have ever worked with talk about customer centricity in one form or another. Perhaps they call it customer proximity, customer understanding, customer focus, being customer driven but the essence is the same. How can you be customer-centric if you have never met one? (Reference my earlier story about managing the voicemail product.) So you really want to run this test yourself as it will help you to develop your own understanding of your customers and/or users.

c) Your idea or 'hunch' at this stage is not well formed. So that means you will need to iterate, making appropriate changes as you learn about your potential customers and/or user groups, what they need and want. You need to be able to make these changes on the spot and that would be very difficult to do if you have to go back through a change process and/or feed that into another party who is standing in between you and the customer. It will cost the organisation much more in staff time to stand between you and the customer, so why not just go direct?!

If you have Insights/Research teams, I would take them through the seven steps of The Really Good Idea Test and explain what you are going to do. You could ask their advice as you work through Step 3 (Create questions) onwards as they are likely to have expertise and good advice. In particular, they could be very helpful on Step 4 (Find interviewees) as they may have existing databases of interviewees or relationships with specialised companies that recruit people for research. Of course, you must share the output with them. They might like you to write up your results and findings in a particular way so that it fits with their existing cataloguing of research results which they can share with the rest of the business. While your ideas are at a super early stage, there are bound to be insights that will be useful to others in the company as you are gathering knowledge about target customer and/or user segments who they may already address now or might do in the future.

How to accept help carrying out the research interviews

If you need or want to draft in other people to help you carry out interviews, you can maintain consistency by giving them a copy of your research script. For example, this would work well with a sales team who can incorporate some research for you while they are in the field with customers. Talk them through your journey from Step 1 (Write hypothesis) and make sure that they pay special attention to Step 6 (Conduct interviews) as there are lots of tips on how to get the most out of research interviews. In particular, make sure that they also record the interviews that they carry out. This does not get you out of doing them though. You will still benefit greatly by doing some yourself!

A note on research regulations and personal safety

Please do check the research-related regulations and legislation for your region/country. It is highly likely that there are regulations and laws governing a range of areas when doing your own research. These differ from country to country. There will be regulations around approaching existing customers for research purposes, for getting permission to carry out research with minors, asking for personal data, ensuring you tell people what you are going to do with data, how you store people's data and so on. I often turn to the Market Research Society who publish a good position for the UK. If you look on their website, you will find a link to the equivalent international organisations. In addition to these, certain industries and sectors, such as health, may have additional regulations that you need to be aware of. So before you start even recruiting any potential interviewees, make sure that you understand the boundaries and best practice.

While I encourage you to carry out The Really Good Idea Test yourselves and to get close to your customers and users, please be careful not to put yourself in any situation which may compromise your safety and note that I do not accept any responsibility for you doing so!

TOP TIPS

The Really Good Idea Test templates will help you to apply the seven steps to your own idea

Get into an iterative mindset, knowing that as you go through the seven steps, you will be going back and forward making improvements

See advice on getting buy-in if you are working in an organisation or with investors

COMMON PITFALLS

Thinking you are too far down the line to go back and check your assumptions about how people think, feel and are going to behave

Being too focused on technology solutions rather than how it can solve a customer problem, need or desire

Not being willing to meet your customers and/or users face-to-face

STEP 1

WRITE HYPOTHESIS

KEY POINTS

Turn your idea into a testable hypothesis that you can put to The Really Good Idea Test

This reframing of your idea will include your goal, who you are going to deliver value for and the action you need those people to take

Get introduced to an example that will be used to explain how to apply the seven steps throughout the test

The first thing to do with your idea is to turn it into a hypothesis that you can put to The Really Good Idea Test. Think of it as a theory, which is a starting point for further investigation. The hypothesis sets out the purpose of your idea and forms the basis of what you are putting to The Really Good Idea Test. By its nature it is a statement of your best guesses based on your theories; after all, if you already knew the answer, you would not need to run it through this test. It is a chance to get all your thoughts onto paper. You will keep returning to, refining and improving on your hypothesis throughout the seven steps.

As well as helping to distil and focus your idea, the hypothesis is also a good way of explaining and summarising what you are trying to achieve not only for yourself but also for other people. You have probably seen a number of different definitions of hypothesis, so for the purposes of this test it is made up of four different parts:

Part 1: Your goal
This is what you are trying to achieve overall.

Part 2: The idea
A short description of what it is you want to create (if you know).

Part 3: The people who will benefit
Reference who has the problem, need or desire that you want to solve or meet.

Part 4: The action
What you need these people to do so you can realise your goal.

In this step I am going to start using some examples, most of which will stay with us throughout all seven steps.

1. Your goal

What are you trying to achieve overall?

Decide what your own personal goal is before you begin working on your new idea. People often refer to this exercise as 'product therapy'. The word 'therapy' comes from the Greek *'therapeuein'* meaning to 'attend, do service, take care of' and this is what I ask of you. Be honest and up front about what you want to achieve and you will do yourself the best service that you can.

It may help to go stand in front of a mirror. Ask yourself what you are really trying to achieve with this new idea and look at yourself right in the eyes. What does success look like to you? Imagine the end state.

Now complete the following statement honestly: 'Through developing this new idea I would like to . . .'.

Here are some example answers:

- . . . meet my annual financial targets
- . . . get a promotion / get the next job / build my CV
- . . . make some money
- . . . save money
- . . . save time
- . . . make this process more efficient
- . . . build my own company
- . . . solve problems for humanity
- . . . find a way to get more funding for more problem solving
- . . . commercialise my research
- . . . be recognised as an entrepreneur
- . . . start a career in business

Some innovators feel uncomfortable talking about money. This often comes up with academics, third sector, social enterprises and charities. Not everyone is innovating to make as big a profit as they possibly can. Some people are doing this for social good or for the good of humanity and yes, personal reward flows from that. They want their efforts to count for something and it matters not whether they actually are going to make any money from it. But someone has to. Very few propositions are funded forever. They need to at least cover their own costs; we all need money to live!

When I work with PhD students, I ask them these teaser questions:

- Are you thinking about how to commercialise your research? Perhaps you wonder how to turn an idea into a commercial product or service?
- Fancy yourself as an innovator?
- Or just want a better understanding of business in practice?
- Perhaps you just want to make the world a better place?

The answers are usually split almost equally between making the world a better place and more commercial, money-related objectives. You can of course have both of those answers. We do need to talk about how money is not a dirty word though. After all, even when making the world a better place, there are likely to be costs to cover. There are many worthy initiatives out there. Look at how they are funded and think about what is going to happen when the money runs out. Somewhere along the line, someone needs to provide funding and customers and/or stakeholders need to see enough benefit, 'value', to keep funding.

Some of the PhD students then recognise that while they are passionate about what they could deliver, they are not motivated by the need to raise funding to commercialise their idea or by being the person that actually brings it to market. So they realise that they need to think about this from their customer's perspective. An organisation may like to work with one of their inventions but they will only do that if they can see that the numbers add up – that there is a viable commercial outcome at some future point. They then start to focus on identifying a paying customer to take their idea forward.

Shifting from thinking about their solution, they can now see that they need to find a business model that will appeal to a paying customer and if they can't, then this is not a good idea at all!

So please define what is going to make you happy before you start out. Define your primary motivation but also be clear that you are at least going to need to break even as well.

Here are some examples of how you can build this into the first part of your hypothesis statement:

- My hypothesis is that we will reduce the incidents of crime in this area if . . .
- My hypothesis is that we can become profitable within a year if . . .
- My hypothesis is that we will establish ourselves as market leader within six months if . . .
- My hypothesis is that I will meet the objectives my boss has set me if . . .
- My hypothesis is that I will be named in a leading industry publication within the next year if . . .
- My hypothesis is that we will reduce the number of heart problems by 2025 if . . .
- My hypothesis is that we will generate new revenues from existing customers in nine months if . . .

Try to make your overall objective specific and measurable. It should feel like an attainable goal. Not only does it help to clarify the overall purpose, it also allows you to put yourself into the picture with total honesty and clarity. As well as being a constant reminder that keeps you focused, it is also very helpful for other people who are working with you to be able to see what your goal is.

If you are doing this for someone else, perhaps for your company or a client, you can also specify that, for example:

My hypothesis is that we will generate revenue for our client in six months if . . .

2. The idea

In short, what is your idea? (There is no need to answer this if you do not yet know).

Being succinct is much more difficult than using lots of words! Imagine you are talking to someone who is not in your social or business circles. What would you say is the core of your idea? Here are some examples that follow on from the start of the hypothesis statement you have worked on above. These examples are intended to show how simple the description can be:

- . . . we implement an improved process
- . . . we launch a new way to . . .
- . . . we run a marketing programme
- . . . we build an app
- . . . we create a new game
- . . . we can find a solution to . . .
- . . . we develop a new technology that . . .

If you do not yet know what the thing is that you are going to create, you can use the more generic examples above like 'we find a solution to', but if you already have a clear idea of what you want to do, now is your chance to add it in.

3. The people who will benefit

Who has the problem, need or desire that you want to solve or meet?

Now we need to identify who is going to benefit from this idea. At this stage, of course, this is going to be guesswork based on your theory, hunches and feelings. Rest assured that through The Really Good Idea Test, we will be finding evidence to support your hunches rather than let you power forward basing your whole proposition around unproven assumptions. So let rip and guess away!

Many product failures are based on a misconception or lack of evidence of what the customer really wants so we must address this right now at the start. I searched the internet to find some statistics around the reasons for product failure, which is generally understood to be that the launched product failed to reach its success metrics (customer numbers, or revenues and so on). Most stats given for overall product failure sit somewhere between 70–90 per cent. When delving into the reasons for failure, the most commonly cited reason is failure to understand value, customer and user needs and failure to work out what they are worth. Neilson, a long-established global market research and data analytics company, describes this as 'neglecting to address a broad consumer need'. So here we are, right at the beginning of this process, thinking about who wants a solution so that we do not create a product or solution that is struggling to find a market.

So please park thoughts that you may be having about what you think you want to deliver. This is not about what you are thinking of building, it is a step before that and asks you to think about how the people you are building the product for might feel, think and behave. This may be a big shift in your thinking. Many innovators get heavily involved in thinking about the solution before they invest time identifying who is going to benefit.

Start off by mapping all the people involved

Having seen the confusion that can be caused in understanding the roles that different groups of people play, I have created the concept of doing a 'people map'. It will help you better identify who you are directly adding value for versus who plays a part in helping you deliver that value.

The first important distinction is to understand the difference between a 'user' and a 'customer'. A user is the one who uses (experiences) the product and the customer will be the one to pay for it. As we discussed in the introduction to this book, somewhere along the line you need to be paid (cash, or in kind) for the solution that you are going to deliver. Throughout this book I refer to 'customer and/or user' to make the distinction clear. They may be the same person, or different people. I have seen innovators address only customers and ignore their users and vice versa. You have to understand the needs of both of these in order to create a successful solution.

This is an example of a scenario that is straightforward as the customer and user are the same person:

Example: Taxi app where the customer is also the user

Let's wind back a few years and think about all those taxi apps. The main usage scenario is the person who uses the service and pays for it is the same, so they are both the customer and the user. There are some obvious circumstances where they are not going to be the same person, for example a host books the taxi for their guest or a younger person for an older non-app-using person, but for the time being, take the likely majority as being a simple transaction between the taxi app and the customer who is also the user. I learnt in my early days of process re-engineering to design for the majority first.

Here are a few scenarios that are not as straightforward as the customer and user are not the same person:

Example: Child's app where the customer and user are different people

A ten-year-old child wants to buy an app that their friend has. Here, the parent is likely to be the customer and the child is the user.

Example: Small company telephone system where the customer and user are different people

A small business manager is in the market for a new telephone system for the office. It is very common in business-to-business sales (where a business is selling to another business) that the user and the customer differ. The employees are the users of the telephone system and the customer could be the small business manager who has the budget to pay for it.

Example: Educational company online study where the customer and user are different people

An education company wants to offer a way to study online rather than at a physical school. Again here, the user is the student so is unlikely to be the person who will be paying. The customer is likely to be the school or a parent.

Take a look at the 'people map' I have completed below for these scenarios. You can see in this 'people map' that the customer can be different to the user. You can also see there could be an important influencer who you may want to consider at some point. Perhaps they are instrumental in your marketing plan to help you reach your target customers. They may not be a priority right now, but they soon will be. There is also a 'Promoter' who I have defined as the person who makes the recommendation to the customer. They could also be considered to be an 'Influencer'. I have called the customer the 'budget holder' as they are the one who holds the purse strings. You can see that in a business scenario, there may be people between you and the budget holder both as the recommender and, once agreed with the customer, as the one who processes the payment. Sometimes the people who play those roles are so influential that you need to think of them as if they are also the customer. They may have the power to block your proposition. Typically, in a business environment, suppliers can find themselves having to get approval from a number of different departments before getting to procurement, who may block a proposal as your organisation does not fit the minimum generic supplier criteria.

PEOPLE MAP	Taxi App	Child's App	Small Company Telephone System	Educational Company Online Study
User	Traveller	Child	Office Manager & Office Staff	Student
Introducer	Traveller's friend	Child's Friend or Parent	Office Admin	School or Friend or Parent
Promoter (recommends to budget holder)	N/A	Child or Other Parent	Office Manager	Teacher or Friend or Student
Customer (budget holder)	Traveller	Parent A or Parent B or Either Parent	CEO	School or Parent
Processes the payment	Traveller	Parent A or Parent B or Either Parent	Office Admin	School Admin or Parent
Beware: Mystery Influencer!	Traveller's friend	Grandparent	Existing Trusted IT Supplier	Friends & Teachers

You can also see here the category of 'mystery influencer'. There are groups of people who you do not expect to have to consider. They are not necessarily positive or negative but they have influence on the customer and/or user. They can suddenly pop up with an interest and you may not even discover them until after you have launched!

By using this 'people map' you may find that some people feature in a number of different boxes and it should help to clarify the role that each are playing. I have seen people realise that distributors (who help deliver your product to your customers) could actually be a customer group in that they could buy your product and then package it up and sell directly to the customer.

See how the 'people map' works for you. You may of course make changes to your first column heading, but try to run through the thinking to find the groups and then think about which you are going to focus on first.

Please note this 'indoor market project' example. I am going to repeatedly use it to show how to apply each of the seven steps as we go through The Really Good Idea Test.

Example: How the 'people map' helped identify customers, users and other groups

A few years ago, I directed a project in a 1920s-built indoor market. The market had slipped from its former glory and there were a very large number of empty shop units. Before we go on here, I am talking about a project, so what was the idea? What was the product? Was it a service? A proposition? The idea was to run a programme of different activities that would result in a commercially viable indoor market. So for my customer, the person paying me, I was offering a service that was going to deliver that outcome. While the programme itself was stuffed full of new ideas which came to life throughout the period, the core offer was a rent-free test trade period with low utility charges and a wraparound programme of marketing that would drive footfall for these early test traders. Success for my customer (the landlord), was to have new traders signed up to longer term, full-rent lease agreements.

PEOPLE MAP	My Agency
User	Potential Market Trader & Market Punter
Introducer	Council
Promoter (recommends to budget holder)	Council & Landlord's Market Manager
Customer (budget holder)	Landlord CEO
Processes the payment	Landlord Finance Director
Beware: Mystery Influencer!	Local Interest Groups & Existing Traders

In this example, the landlord is my direct customer; they are paying me and as they are a business, there are quite a few different departments and individuals involved. You can see that there is a market manager who works for the landlord and has influence with our customer, the landlord's CEO. The finance director in this case is processing payments, so there are some procurement hoops to jump through but no need to address them as a high priority group.

The potential new permanent traders are one of the user groups. While they are not giving me money directly, they are going to be the main actor in the plan. If we are not able to find test traders, there will be none to convert to permanent, and the plan will fail.

Another vital group are the market punters. People who are going to be customers of the market traders who are, en masse, the footfall. The indoor market experience is being created for them to enjoy. Without paying punters in the market, without an audience, there is no project success. They therefore are also my users and are, of course, the traders' customers as they will be spending money with them. Without this group there is no chance I can deliver on the landlord proposition.

The council introduced us to the market landlords and they had a big influence with our customer, continuing to provide

support throughout the programme. Moving forward into the project, they were able to provide really valuable support such as offering reduced rates to test traders, granting licences for events and extended hours and spreading the word through marketing. So as an 'introducer', it is really useful to write a value proposition for them so that you understand their needs as a basis to create and maintain a good working relationship.

There were a lot of vocal local interest groups, bloggers who reached large audiences and many different community groups representing the melting pot of different cultures who lived in the area. We spent a lot of time working with those groups to understand what their needs, problems and desires were and trying to deliver to their expectations too. It felt as if they had the capability to derail the project. We did not really know they existed until we started. They are a good example of 'mystery influencers'.

There were a few existing market traders, a lot of whose shop units had been passed down through their family line. They included a butcher, restaurant, cookware shop, a wig seller and a grocer. These traders had a few loyal customers but they were worried about how they would continue. This group were also 'mystery influencers' as we assumed they would embrace activities to drive footfall. We realised that we had made incorrect assumptions about them once we started executing the project.

There were some other groups who turned out to be instrumental to the success of the project. We worked out that it was not tenable to expect the shop units to be occupied with potential traders at all times and we also wanted to bring the space back as a destination for the community. Both of these elements lead us to realise how important artists and community groups, social enterprises and charities were to help bring the indoor market back to life and give it both a useful and dynamic presence. They are 'mystery influencers' as well as many also being 'users' as they are market punters.

Now you can prioritise the different groups of people

In most cases, you will put your direct customer as the first priority as they are the ones paying you. Below, we take the example of the indoor market project and work through how prioritisation can work.

Example: Prioritising different customers, users and other groups of people in the indoor market project

In this case, my customer's success (the landlord) was entirely dependent on the success of their test trade tenants and, in turn, the test trade tenants were entirely dependent on the market punters spending money in their shops. The priority in this case would be to find potential test traders who were also interested in a longer term lease and secondly to drive footfall from the market punters. So those two user groups, the test traders and the market punters, are the highest priority.

The council were an important stakeholder and were the next in the priority list. Although they did not pay us directly, their support was really important.

The existing traders were next, and soon after launch, the local interest groups made themselves known and as a mystery influencer were promoted upwards in the priority list, sharpish!

We had a vision of the marketplace as a destination site that felt, as the Greek 'agora' would have, a place to meet, learn, socialise, share, be entertained, not just for trade. Our desire to embrace all that the community had to offer was fundamental to this vision. The interest groups, existing traders along with artists, social enterprises and charities were a core part of that. (Some of the artists, social enterprises and charities did fall into the bucket of being test traders and were able to build sustainable ongoing concerns as well as benefit from deliberately temporary tenancies and pop-up appearances.) These groups were so important to how we measured our own personal success, even if they were not a priority for our landlord customer's commercial success.

The point I make for The Really Good Idea Test is that if you end up with a number of different groups of people, you need to think through them one by one, work out what role they play and then list them in priority order. You can reflect the priorities of all the different groups in this section of your hypothesis statement. Have a go at prioritising the different groups in your 'people map'.

Finally, create value propositions for each of the different groups of people

You may have heard the term 'value proposition'. Broadly speaking it lays out the case for why a customer should buy from you, and it asks you to start with the customer and/or user and their problem. It is a sentence that explains the purpose and value of your idea. If you can quantify the value it will really help to explain and progress the idea. It is a vital exercise in enabling you to identify the people who will benefit in your overall hypothesis statement.

The term 'value proposition' is used in a number of different contexts, but commonly, it is a supposition, (proved or not), of where you think you can deliver something of merit, worth, usefulness, desirability or benefit. All of these words are synonyms of the word 'value' so, just like your goal, value does not need to just be about money. The value proposition will also get you thinking about delivering value over and above what is already available so that you do not take on competitors who would be difficult to beat and fight for market space where there is none.

You are likely to find yourself putting a lot of thought into how you are going to express your idea as a value proposition, and that is good. Crafting this statement will push you to focus on the things that are important right now and to leave aside the things that are not. This exercise should be cathartic. It is going to make you feel good as you need to write down all your guesses, hunches and thoughts. Do not worry about whether you have evidence for what you say or not, or whether what you say is right or wrong. Just let it flow!

The value proposition statement is not only the starting point for everything you do, but it also needs to stay with you (and evolve if need be) as you work through your solution design right through to your go-to-market plans. It will keep you true to the customer and/ or user and serve as a constant reminder of the benefit you promised you will deliver. Keep it up to date and by your side at all times!

Example: Value proposition for the landlord of the indoor market, showing explanation for each prompt to complete

Prompt to complete	Example	Explanation
FOR	the landlord of the indoor market	Who has the need/ problem/desire?
WHO	has a very high proportion of empty shops in their loss-making indoor market	What problem/need/ desire do they have that you think you can solve?
OUR	programme to bring the indoor market back to viability	What generic product/ service category does this fall into?
GIVES	shop rental revenues within six months, a reduction in pressure from the local council (that results from crime associated with aban-doned buildings) and reduces further costly dilapidation as those cur-rently empty shops will have active caretakers	What benefit can you deliver them?
UNLIKE	today's situation where the market runs at a loss every day with increasing crime, no funds for the upkeep of the building and poor future prospects	How does it differ from / improve upon what is available today?

Guidance on writing value proposition statements
'FOR' – Who has the need / problem / desire?

Who is the beneficiary of your idea? Each of the different groups of people you have identified need their own value proposition statement. Once you have written them, you may find that they are similar and so you can bring them back together later on, but do start off by building them separately or it could get messy! So in the example for the indoor market project, the landlord's value proposition statement needs to be different from the potential test trader, which is different from the existing market trader and so on.

Forcing yourself to consider each customer and user segment separately will ensure that you don't overlook what each needs and wants. Here is an easier example, where the customer and the user are the same person:

Example: Value proposition for a new taxi app idea where customer and user are the same person

For existing taxi and app users **who** find their existing taxi services are unreliable **our** app **gives** them a way to be able to track their driver's arrival time and location in real time, **unlike** today where they can be left waiting without any information.

So what about the taxi app? The answer seems pretty straight forward in terms of being a customer and/or user as they are the same person. Do you notice that I called them 'Existing taxi users and app users'? This is a further high-level descriptor and it can be useful. In this case, they are not just people who want to get from A to B as those people may like to walk or take public transport. They are people who are already happy with taking taxis and are familiar with apps. If you do not add these high-level descriptors, you may find yourself trying to persuade people who take public transport today to convert to taking taxis and that would completely change your value proposition. Your problem and benefits offerings would be different. Similarly, it is good to focus on people already using apps. If they are not, then they do not fall into your target segment and you will find yourself trying to write a value proposition statement about why they should use an app at all and this will distract you from your focus.

So you can consider these existing taxi users and app users to be your first, most addressable segment. While I encourage you to add a high-level descriptor if it feels helpful, try not to get into too much detail at this stage. We will get into this later when we look at the different groups we need to research with. For now, separate out the high-level user from the high-level customer but try not to end up with too many user and customer segments.

You have a choice to make at this early stage which affects how you write the remainder of the value proposition and subsequently what you are going to put to The Really Good Idea Test.

'WHO' – What problem / need / desire do they have that you think you can solve?

Focus on what problem, need or desire you think those people would tell you that they have, not what problem you (as the solution designer) want them to have. Remember, at this stage, not to worry about whether you have evidence or not as this is all about your hunches and what you think.

The landlord's problem in the indoor market project example is that they have empty shop units so they are currently making a loss. In the taxi app example given above, they are trying to get from A to B in a taxi and you can just hear them tell you about their last taxi experience when they were left waiting or had to keep calling the taxi office for updates.

A common mistake that innovators make is they would say that the existing taxi and app users want an efficient app or that the indoor market landlord wants a project to bring the market back to life. This skips straight to the solution that the innovator wants to provide them with, rather than the problem, need or desire that they actually have. If you do this, you will start to test the solution and skip all the investigation into whether the customer and/or user has the problem, need or desire that you think they have.

Another way to think about the 'who' part of the value proposition is to think about the job that the beneficiary is trying to get done. The example below of a gaming app for children demonstrates this point very clearly. You can also see, looking further into the value proposition statement, that the 'gives' part responds directly to the 'who' part as that is where the benefits are answering the problem.

Example: The job to be done for a gaming app from a child and a parent's point of view is quite different

For a child **who** needs some distraction while their parent's attention is elsewhere, **our** gaming app **gives** them hours of entertainment, **unlike** a physical game where they may still want someone to play with and where they may get bored more quickly.

For the busy parent **who** needs to keep their child occupied so they can get on with necessary household chores, **our** new mobile game **gives** the child an educational experience that will engage them for hours, **unlike** other games which may not be as educational; finding a minder which requires time for you to organise and other physical games that may create further mess.

'OUR' – What generic product/service category does this fall into?

Think about what your category is. A common mistake is to start describing what you have either too technically or in a feature-based or 'salesy' way. So, avoid statements like 'our brilliant new colourful and engaging experience' and try to look at this objectively. Perhaps it helps to think about what you would search for if you were looking for it online. Or how you might describe it to someone from Mars (that is someone who doesn't know anything about it!).

For example, in the indoor market project, the landlords are being offered a 'programme to bring the indoor market back to viability': pretty much does what it says on the tin. It is a programme of activity that is being offered. In the taxi app example, it is simply an 'app'. There is no sales fluff – that is what it is!

'GIVES' – What benefit can you deliver them?

What response can you deliver to the customer to alleviate their pain, need or desire? What benefits do they want to gain from a solution? Here, you need to avoid writing a list of product features that they don't even know they want. Instead, focus on the bigger picture.

In the indoor market project example, the landlords are being offered 'shop rental revenues within six months, a reduction in pressure from the local council (that results from crime associated with abandoned buildings) and a reduction in upkeep costs as those currently empty shops will have active caretakers'. You can see how these relate directly to having empty shop units.

They are being offered a chance to get those shops rented out, which is the key to them addressing the additional problems – the pressure from the council and the cost to keep those empty shops in a good condition. These are the real benefits that they need from a solution that sits under this GIVES part of the value proposition.

In the taxi app example, the customer problem (as explained further in the 'unlike' section) is about unreliability and the 'gives' response is directly related to that: 'A way to see their driver's arrival time and location in real time'. Is this a list of features? Not really, it is a way to describe what relief you can give to their pain. Now it just so happens that there are many other features that are likely to be highly valued too. For example, you can order the taxi via the app which is much easier that trying to be heard when you are in a loud environment; locations for you and the driver are automatically captured; the price will be the same or less than existing services; you pay through the app; you can see and add ratings for drivers; you can share cabs with others bringing the price down and so on. However, at this stage, the pain of actually getting the taxi to arrive is what we have chosen to work.

It is advisable to just start with that main problem first. If this benefit does not make it through the test, then move on to one of those other problems and revise your value proposition statement accordingly.

Let's talk about money again: I have not used 'cheaper' as a relevant benefit in any of these examples. Now if you do have something that is going to be cheaper than the current solution(s) and you think that price is the most important motivator, then do include it in the value proposition statement. Price is often the only remaining differentiator in a commoditised market. For example, mobile phone service provision is now so commoditised that you see advertising leading with price claims like how much data is included in the package. Price wars can frankly just be boring and difficult to win (especially for new entrants to the market or smaller businesses), which is why you see advertising in these markets leading on lifestyle benefits, with loyalty schemes and rewards that have nothing to do with the product or service. Are you in that space? Can you avoid at this point building price in as a major value factor? If not, then go on, add it in but please be cautious if you are using 'cheaper' as a default benefit every time.

'UNLIKE' – How does it differ from / improve upon what is available today?

There are two parts to this section:

(a) Who is offering solutions to this problem today?

(b) How satisfactory do you think their existing solutions are?

With the taxi app example, there are other taxi companies who are direct competitors. We know from the earlier part of the value proposition statement that those other taxis can be unreliable, and we know from the latter part of the value proposition statement (in the 'unlike' part) that customers can be left waiting without any information.

In the indoor market project example, the 'unlike' part of the landlord's value proposition is 'unlike today's situation where the market runs at a loss every day with increasing crime, no funds for the upkeep of the building and poor future prospects'. This is a very important example to use for helping to understand the 'unlike' part of the value proposition it shows a 'do nothing' situation. The alternative in this case, is that the situation remains as is. There are no other offers or solutions on the table other than the status quo.

This 'unlike' part of the value proposition is a real good leveller. If you think you can provide a solution that is better than what you think exists today, then you are on to something! Remember, once again, that this all about what you think, not necessarily what you know.

Tip: Stand in each person's shoes to write their specific value proposition

You can see that there are different ways of writing the value proposition statement and how just one word can change its direction. The most important point here is to understand what job the person is trying to get done and, based on that, what general solutions are available to them to get that job done today. Perhaps they use a solution that is premade by someone else; perhaps it is one they have put together themselves; perhaps there is no solution available at all. If there is no viable solution being offered today then your unlike statement needs to reflect that, spelling out the impact of that scenario.

My best advice is to write a number of value proposition statements. Play around with them, changing the words you use and see how that affects the remainder of the statement. Exhaust all those thoughts in your head, get all those hunches down on paper and see how they fit together. See what feels right to you and which words best capture the essence of your thoughts. If you need to split up your thoughts into a few different statements, then that is fine. The value proposition is a living statement so you can evolve and adapt it as you go.

If you end up with a number of value proposition statements, you can put each one to The Really Good Idea Test and see which fares the strongest. If your user and/or customer segments are the same, then you may be able to test more than one value proposition in one research conversation.

To conclude, writing these different value propositions is an exercise in empathy. When you step into the beneficiary's shoes you will find the viewpoint of the value proposition changes.

Going back to the indoor market project example, we can see that there are differences between the different value propositions and how actually writing one can refocus how you write another, as they are all related:

Example: Value proposition for the potential test traders in the indoor market project

For potential new permanent traders **who** have a new shop idea, **our** free test trading period in one of the indoor market's empty shops **gives** a rent-free, reduced rates low-commitment opportunity to see what works, with the additional sales and marketing benefits of being part of a larger overall project, **unlike** other retail opportunities which are mostly standalone and require a commitment to longer term leases with rent and full rates payments chargeable from the outset.

Example: Value proposition for the potential market visitors (punters) in the indoor market project

For market punters, initially local people, **who** are looking for ways to spend their leisure time, **our** indoor market full of ever-changing activities, pop ups and new test-trading retailers **gives** a new, eclectic shopping, dining, community, multi-cultural and creative experience, **unlike** other usual haunts where you know what you are going to get every time.

Example: Value proposition for the council in the indoor market project

For the council **who** is under increasing pressure from the government to reduce vacant retail units and counteract the negative effects of falling consumer confidence in a time of recession **our** empty shops programme **gives** a way to address to reduce the negative effects of empty retail spaces on the community (both eyesore and crime related) and support new local business, **unlike** previous ideas that had not tackled the issue effectively enough.

Example: Value proposition for the existing market traders in the indoor market project

For existing market traders **who** want to continue to run their own viable shop, **our** empty shops programme to bring the indoor market back to viability, **gives** them an opportunity to increase their revenues and make their businesses more sustainable through increased market footfall and potential sales to new test trading tenants and the organisers of pop-up projects, **unlike** today where despite servicing a core of loyal customers, overall footfall is in decline resulting in a threat to their long-term viability.

Example: Value proposition for artists in the indoor market project

For artists **who** want to display their art, show their performance, get some publicity, test out new ideas, reach new audiences, entertain existing audiences, generate revenue (if desired) and build up their portfolio, **our** 'pop-up' space **gives** a free short-term space with sales and marketing opportunities, **unlike** other opportunities that may not have the publicity potential or free space on offer.

Example: Value proposition for the social enterprises and charities in the indoor market project

For social enterprises and charities **who** want to get some publicity, test out new ideas, increase traction with the public and generate revenue (if desired), **our** free test trading period in one of the indoor market's empty shops and / or 'pop-up' space **gives** a free short-term space with sales and marketing opportunities, **unlike** other opportunities that may not have the publicity potential or free space on offer.

4. The action

What do you need those people to do so you can realise your goal?

This is the final element of your hypothesis statement and something that is often overlooked. Be clear about what you need them to do: Spend money? Register? Download an app? Switch providers? Sign a contract? Focus on what you need from them in return for the value that you are going to deliver to them. This part needs to be action-orientated. If you can create enough value for a beneficiary or beneficiaries, then they will take a particular action, which will mean that you can deliver on your overall objective. If they don't take this action, then it must be that their need is not great enough, or the benefit is not strong enough, which means that you do not have a powerful enough value proposition.

Bring it all together to write your hypothesis

Now the challenge is to bring all four of these parts together: Part 1: Your goal + 2: The idea + Part 3: The people who will benefit + Part 4: The action.

You need to express the hypothesis as a positive statement rather than a negative as that makes it easier to test. You will also feel better about it! Make it as simple a statement as you can.

Here is an example for the potential test traders in the indoor market project. It shows how to bring the four elements together in quite a complicated scenario. It is more complex as there are a few 'actions' here and three different groups of people: the landlord, the trader and the market punter.

Example: Hypothesis for potential test traders in the indoor market project

(Reminder of value proposition: **For** potential new permanent traders **who** have a new shop idea, **our** free test trading period in one of the indoor market's empty shops **gives** a rent-free, reduced rates low-commitment opportunity to see what works, with the additional sales and marketing benefits of being part of a larger overall project, **unlike** other retail opportunities which are mostly standalone and require a commitment to longer term leases with rent and full rates payments chargeable from the outset.)

Our hypothesis is that we can generate full-price rentals in six months from all twenty empty shops if the right mix of traders are given free test trading opportunities within a broader programme of activity.

Here is a breakdown of that hypothesis to see how all four elements are included:

- Goal: To generate the landlord full-price rentals for from all twenty empty shops in six months.

- Idea: To give free test trading opportunities within a broader programme of activity.

- People who will benefit: The landlords who eventually get full-price rentals and the potential test traders, who get to test out if they can afford to rent a shop unit.

- Action: The potential test traders take up free test trading opportunities and can generate enough revenue from market punters to be able to afford the full-price rentals.

Here you can see the overall objective to get all twenty shops leased out at full price. It may not be those same test traders who take up those units, but they will all be rented out at full price. We know that the landlord is the main beneficiary but the traders and punters also benefit from free test trading and from the enjoyment of a revived marketplace. There are a few actions here: The taking up of test trading and the signing up of full-price rentals and the market punters who need to shop. (You can state the hypothesis as 'my' or 'our' hypothesis.)

Here is another hypothesis from the taxi app example. This one is more straightforward and shows that the overall objective is to generate revenue, the idea is to build an app, the beneficiaries are existing taxi and app users and the action you need them to take is to download and start using the app.

Example: Hypothesis for taxi app project

(Reminder of the value proposition: **For** existing taxi and app users **who** find their existing taxi services are unreliable **our** app **gives** them a way to be able to track their driver's arrival time and location in real time, **unlike** today where they can be left waiting without any information.)

My hypothesis is that there is an opportunity to generate revenue within a year, if we create a new taxi app for existing taxi and app users to download that shows drivers' arrival times and location in real time.

Do bear in mind that of course there are a number of different ways you can craft the hypothesis. As long as they contain those four elements in a succinct manner then that is fine. You will have the opportunity to iterate and improve upon your hypothesis at any stage throughout this test.

Completing The Really Good Idea Test templates

- -

Are you working on your own idea as you go through this book?
If so, then have a go for yourself using the CORE template.

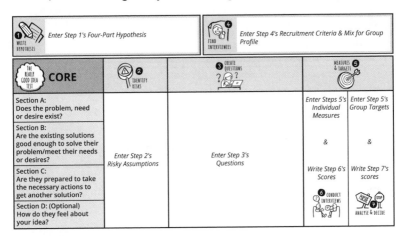

Remember that you can download these templates from
productdoctor.co.uk.

Right now, you are now on Step 1 (Write hypothesis) and you are
ready to write your hypothesis into the highlighted Step 1 box.

CORE template showing Step 1's box

What do I write in this box?

Just write in your hypothesis. Here is an example of a complete Step 1 box for the indoor market project example:

1 WRITE HYPOTHESIS

Our hypothesis is that we can generate full-price rentals in 6 months from all 20 empty shops if the right mix of traders are given free test trading opportunities within a broader programme of activity

Try it for yourself!

Remember you can download the template from productdoctor.co.uk

TOP TIPS

Use a 'people map' to help you distinguish customers from users and other groups of people

Write 'value propositions' for each of the most important groups of people to help you identify problems, need and/or desires for your hypothesis

Start to adopt a focus on people who you can add value for, not solutions or features you can deliver

COMMON PITFALLS

Failing to differentiate between customers and users (and other involved groups)

Failing to focus on the suspected problems, desires and needs that exist for customers and users

Writing a hypothesis that is technical, feature-based or salesy rather than benefits-focused

STEP ②

IDENTIFY RISKS

KEY POINTS

Identify where you have a lack of evidence on high-impacting elements of your hypothesis

Spend time carrying out some desk research to see if there is any other evidence that already exists

Categorise your riskiest assumptions against the four main sections of risk

Many innovators fail to recognise that their early-stage assumptions may contain different levels of risk and likelihood. In some cases, they think these cannot be addressed until the product or service is launched. Well they can! In this step we will look at identifying risky assumptions at an early stage.

A risky assumption exists where there is something of high impact to the success of the idea and where evidence is low, so they are likely to be the elements that you will feel the most uncomfortable about. The riskiest assumptions will be those things that keep you awake at night as they could cause your whole business model to fail. They are the things that can trip you up later on, once you have spent time and money developing your idea and there is no need for this to be the case.

In this step, we make sure that the riskiest assumptions are uncovered, rather than burying our heads in the sand. Once we find them, we write questions in Step 3 (Create questions,) for carefully profiled group(s) of customers and/or users who we find in Step 4 (Find interviewees), which will get evidence for or against each of those assumptions.

Four main categories of risky assumptions

In nearly all the early idea tests that I run, the riskiest assumptions map into four sections (labelled A, B, C and D). You can use these sections as a shortcut and a checklist for identifying the risks in your idea. You will see that the sections are a natural follow-on to the work that you have already done in your Step 1 (Write hypothesis) work. These are the four sections of risk:

Section A: Does the problem, need or desire exist? Is there a group of people who have the problem/need/desire that you think they do? Are you right about the benefits that they are looking to get from a solution?

Section B: Are the existing solutions good enough to solve their problem/meet their needs or desires? Is the problem/

need/desire big enough for them to be looking for a different solution? Are your thoughts about the competition and the (value proposition 'unlike') landscape correct? Is there an opportunity for another player in this market?

Section C: Are they prepared to take the necessary actions to get another solution? Will they put their time, effort, money or other action towards adopting a different solution?

Section D: (Optional) How do they feel about your idea? Is your current thinking about a solution on track? (if you have got that far)

Section D is optional for those people who have progressed their thinking already. It is fine if you have not started thinking through your solutions yet but for those who have, you will be in front of customers and/or users so it would be daft not to get some feedback if you have time after you have gone through A to C.

If you look at sections A to C in particular, you will see that they are all high impact. That is to say that if your assumptions were not right, then the whole idea could fail.

Prioritising and finding existing evidence

Prioritise the assumptions that have the highest impact

Ask the question: 'If our assumption is wrong, what would the impact be on the success of our idea?' You can choose from three answers:

- HIGH (H) This idea is not going to fly
- MEDIUM (M) Could be problematic but this is not yet an idea killer
- LOW (L) Does not feel too dramatic at this stage

If you are answering 'low', then you do not need to address the assumptions at this stage. You may be in the weeds and getting bogged down in unnecessary detail. If you are answering 'medium' then you could include them in here if you do feel particularly uncomfortable, but they could be left until a bit later on. If you are answering 'high' then yes, you must include them now!

No medium or high risks? Think again

If you honestly feel that you have no medium or high risks then you should already be confidently building and delivering your idea . . . but you are not, you are reading this book! It is very common for innovators to take their new ideas to market with risky assumptions that they could have reduced before getting that far. So perhaps it is worth considering whether you are being too optimistic on your scoring. Put your low-risk items into the four categories and go through the test. Every time I carry out research, I learn something that surprises me.

Do not focus on solutions (D) before the underserved problems, needs and desires (A to C)

Please avoid putting too high a risk rating on assumptions that are related to how to deliver solutions at this stage. Right now, it is far more important to make sure that there is a target user and/or customer with an unmet or underserved problem, need or desire before getting into the detail of the solution. A customer and/or user may love your solution, but they may not have the need or desire for it so you could end up with a great product or service with no market.

You can see that in section D, you get an opportunity to test out your early ideas, but not before you cover sections A to C.

Of course, some ideas have a certain technology or solution-based element at its heart so there will be some technology-related assumptions that need working on. This will be the case where you are working with a particular technology and trying to find the best user cases for it. Take the taxi app example, the idea is all about using an app and the functionality that it can offer to a customer, so the fact that the customer is already an app user and prepared to use the relevant functionality is most important.

It is too early to identify timeframes and cost to build as risks

I have seen innovators get very hung up around whether they can deliver their idea in a certain timeframe, or to a particular budget. This is a major distraction at this early stage. It is likely that you will not have evidence of the customer need and desire yet, so how can you know whether it is feasible to deliver the solution within twelve months?! Allowing yourself to go down this path will also tempt you into doing a business case, which again, is too early to do as you won't have your solution designed so you won't know how much it will cost to deliver.

Spend time trying to find existing evidence

I often find innovators planning to carry out research for evidence that already exists. What a waste of time! So it is worth spending some time digging around first to see what evidence already exists to answer the high- and medium-impact questions you have raised. Perhaps you have some useful information from previous research that has already been carried out, if not by you, by someone else? It is time to do some good desk research to find any evidence that already exists.

Search like mad! Use all search mechanisms available to you on the internet. Is there any published research where you could find some answers? This could be data from professional research and insights companies or publications from industry specialist groups, published demographic data, press articles and so on. Are there other products, services or solutions that are in your space? What can you find people saying about them online? Google Scholar is great for academic papers that are full of references you can dig in to. Following references from reports in mainstream media is very useful as they often summarise and cherry pick information.

Example: Online research for evidence on the indoor market project

An internet search on 'empty shops report' revealed a wealth of data in numerous reports that are based on data from very reputable well-known research and insights analysts. A search on 'empty shops projects' reported the growing trend for artists using empty premises for exhibition and performance. A search on the area's demographics and local economy led to reports commissioned by the council sharing all sorts of useful information. One could find the amount of new shops opening and the number of shops closing that helped to find out more about local traders and so on. You can see how all this data was valuable evidence for this project.

Learn from what has gone before. Have any other companies or competitors shared insights about their experiences, successes or failures? Check blogs, articles, business books and so on. For example, if you are looking at opening a restaurant, there are many examples that have been written about. In particular, you will find a lot from high-profile entrepreneurs who love to share their stories. There are plenty of people who write about their and other people's successes and failures. Learn from them. Talk to people who've tried it before. (I worked with someone once who said that it did not matter what you did, but what you wrote about what you did.) Maybe this will help you also work out whether the environment has changed and you can do better now. Filter out what you think applies and what doesn't.

Despite all this good learning, you need to be careful about applying it directly from one customer segment to another, as you cannot assume that all people will behave in the same way. Here is an example of how it could be dangerous to assume UK users may be the same as US users.

Example: Education company wants to launch successful US product in the UK

An education provider already had a successful online education offering in the US. A lot of the assumptions were absolutely going to be applicable to the UK; for example, around how best to keep students engaged. However, there were some differences that also posed many questions about how different the reception by a UK audience would be. To start with, the education system is quite different in the UK compared with the US. Then there are geographic differences that affect how children are used to studying. The US is around forty times the size of the UK and the UK is roughly eight times more densely populated than the US which will affect all sorts of physical versus online behaviour.

If you do find that your idea already exists, don't give up! It is still worth taking it through the test. In fact, it is quite comforting to see that another innovator also thinks that there is an opportunity! Maybe there is room for another player? Remember that those who are first to market in the short term are often not market leaders in the mid to long term.

Ask people around you if they have any evidence. Put the call out! I am not suggesting that you share your whole hypothesis or post your entire value proposition out to the big wide world; instead I am suggesting that you can ask some choice people from your professional and social circles whether they have any insight that they can share to support a particular element. Particularly in larger companies, there is often a wealth of evidence if you just ask the right people. There is so much insight held in pockets all over larger organisations and I see so much repetition where the research is duplicated to get evidence that already exists.

Here is a great story about digging for and discovering evidence internally which totally changed our direction of travel. It helps to show that data may be more available than we think.

Story: New internal evidence totally changed marketing campaigns to drive mobile phone picture messaging usage

It was a year after mobile picture messaging launched in the UK. The usage figures were way below what was projected. The second wave of camera-phones had arrived, so the camera quality was not bad and market penetration of those phones was at a level where our targets should have been possible. Around the company there were lots of theories about why people were not sending messages, but I needed to get some evidence.

My team embarked on some research. More casually, as we were out and about, we all observed strangers and our own social groups. We found that people were taking photos and showing them to each other but they were not sending them.

We carried out some street interviews with a short questionnaire. We were near a university so were close to a traditionally early adopting group of people. We found that they were not sending photos as it cost to send them and they were watching their pennies.

But here was the big discovery: I discussed this quandary with the business analysts who mined data from the customer call records. We thought maybe there were some answers there around usage patterns and so on. We discovered something that blew our minds: More picture messages contained GIFs (graphic interchange formats) than JPEGs (which are a format for compressing image files). Photos taken on the phone were all presented as JPEGs but the majority were GIFs which were animated or static images that had been created elsewhere. This was totally missed in the observation and interviews as we were so busy looking at photo-taking and sending.

Further research told us that usage was around expressing emotions (note the current popularity of emojis) and key events were a time when people sent these GIFs to each other.

So we sourced a whole range of content from birthday cards to seasonal greetings and 'I'm sorry' to 'give us a kiss'. Within these categories, we also found out that 'edgy' content was popular, so I famously had the management board sign off to 'Bondage Santa' whose cartoon walked onto the screen and opened his cloak to reveal. . .

We then flooded the camera-phone customer base with free animated content encouraging them to send it on, with a promotion that they could send their first five for free.

The result of what we did in response to this evidence got us to the highest number of messages being sent of all networks in the UK, despite having third place in overall customer numbers.

If we had not found all of this out, we would have spent time and money on campaigns to get people sending photos, when the real key to driving the revenue line was pre-created content. The risky assumption was that the customer desire was around sharing photos they had taken when actually the bigger desire was to express emotions and entertain each other, particularly given the quality of the cameras at the time.

While we did manage to boost usage, picture messaging has never really taken off in the way we expected. It was the quality of the photos, the difficulty receiving messages (as there were some user experience issues) and the price per message that were the main restricting factors for people sending photos. In time, one could send photos through instant messaging and upload them on social media sites. These were charged as data, as part of a customer's data allowance, not as a cost per message. They also were sent and received using a different technology and by that time, the cameras had also significantly improved on the phones. Social media has tapped into the whole broadcast behaviour and people now share photos publicly in a way that we had not seen before. And now, we only wish they would just stop!

What constitutes good enough evidence?

I often get asked how to work out if you have sufficient evidence or not. This is, of course, a judgement call. There is no scientific formula I can give you. Perhaps imagine yourself in front of the toughest CEO or investor. Do you feel comfortable enough with the evidence you have to forge ahead? Does it keep you awake at night? Numbers are of course good, but not always possible. I often work with innovators who can't give me the exact numbers but, for example, they hear a problem regularly enough to be sure that it is a large enough problem to address. They will tell me that they hear something consistently from calls to customer services; it is consistently in feedback from sales people and it always comes up in satisfaction surveys. Well that is good enough for me – that is probably a low-risk assumption. Ask them whether they could sleep at night knowing that time and money is going to be spent developing a solution based on the evidence they have provided, and their response will help you work out whether the evidence is good enough!

Even if you have some evidence for the highest riskiest assumptions, you may still feel that you should gather some more. If they are risky enough, then they will be worth double checking. In this table you will see how impact and evidence work together. You can plot your assumptions in this table to check the level of risk that you assign.

RISK ASSESSMENT	Sufficient evidence	Insufficient evidence
High impact	Medium-risk assumption	High-risk assumption
Medium impact	Low-risk assumption	Medium-risk assumption
Low impact	Low-risk assumption	Low-risk assumption

Using this process to manage other people's opinions

Before we move on, I want to explain that this step provides a great opportunity to include hypotheses from other people if they have given you any opinions to date, or if you want to continue to get their buy-in to The Really Good Idea Test's seven-step approach. I often hear from innovators (and have of course experienced first-hand) about the many views and opinions of others they work with. Surely not – a senior management team with a strong opinion?! In a venture of more than one person, this is kind of inevitable. There are always lots of opinions about what this idea should do, what it could be, who it is for and so on. Right now, you have a great opportunity to speak with your colleagues, investors and so on, and get their input to this process of identifying risky assumptions.

Here is an example of how that conversation can play out. The context for this idea is that you are looking at developing a way for school-based students to study a subject online. The theme here is pretty common: You get a point of view which is based on a sample of one customer and/or user who is close to the opinion-holder!

How to handle a typical conversation (using the online study idea at the educational company)

You: You have said before that you do not think many fourteen-to sixteen-year-olds would want to study a subject in an online environment. Why do you think that?

Your colleague: Because my kids told me they wouldn't like to miss out on the social bits of learning a subject in the classroom.

You: Ah ok, so do you know any other kids of that age who also feel the same way? Perhaps who are from a different segment to your kids?

Your colleague: Yes, I asked a few of their friends that were over at the weekend.

You: I think that is an important hypothesis to test as we don't want to get too far down the line and find out that our target users are not going to want to study online. I am going through a process right now of capturing all these important hypotheses from around the business and working out whether we have enough evidence to validate or invalidate them. Where we do not have enough evidence, I am going to go and get that evidence. Do you think that you have a broad enough bank of evidence for this hypothesis or do you think we should get some more?

The chances are that they will suggest you get some more evidence. You have seeded in their mind that even if they have heard it strongly from their own kids and their friends, while they could represent a segment, there are surely not representative enough of all fourteen to sixteen year olds?

It may be that you feel their hypothesis or fear is not quite as high a priority as something else, but if the challenge is causing you any discomfort (for example, this could be from your line manager or an important internal stakeholder), it may be that you give it a higher priority and tackle it right now.

Examples of riskiest assumptions

Here is an example of a set of risky assumptions using the indoor market project, focusing on the potential test traders. In this example, they are all high impact and there is very little evidence in existence, so they are the riskiest.

They are mapped to the four main categories of risk which you will see described in sections A, B, C and D. These four categories form a structure that you continue to work with through the rest of the test.

Four main categories of risk	Risky assumptions
Section A: Does the problem, need or desire exist?	That they want a longer term retail space to sell their offering
Section B: Are the existing solutions good enough to solve their problem / meet their needs or desires?	That the existing ways to sell could be improved upon
Section C: Are they prepared to take the necessary actions to get another solution?	1) Prepared to invest time and money into a new sales opportunity 2) Prepared for continual changing environment, trial and error
Section D: (Optional) How do they feel about your idea?	1) Shop units are appealing 2) Terms, conditions and costs are acceptable

Here is another example using the taxi app idea.

Four main categories of risk	Risky assumptions
Section A: Does the problem, need or desire exist?	That they have a problem with taxis being unreliable
Section B: Are the existing solutions good enough to solve their problem / meet their needs or desires?	That the pain is big enough for them to try something new
Section C: Are they prepared to take the necessary actions to get another solution?	That they are prepared to use a different taxi company
Section D: (Optional) How do they feel about your idea?	That they are positive about ideas on how it would work and what they would be charged

Completing The Really Good Idea Test templates

Are you working on your own idea as you go through this book?

If so, then you should still be using the CORE template. Remember that you can download these templates from productdoctor.co.uk.

At this point, you should have already completed Step 1 (Write hypothesis), which you can see is shaded. Steps 3 to 5 are also shaded as you are not there yet.

You are ready to complete Step 2 (Risky assumptions) which is highlighted.

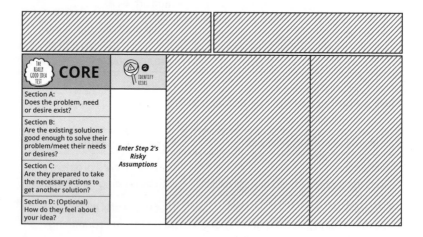

What do I write in this box?

Just write in your risks under each section. If you have more than one main risk in a section, it is a good idea to number them within the section as you want to address them individually as you move forward. Here you can see how to complete the Step 2 box with the indoor market project example.

THE REALLY GOOD IDEA TEST **CORE**	**2** IDENTIFY RISKS
Section A: **Does the problem, need or desire exist?**	*That they want a longer term retail space to sell their offering*
Section B: **Are the existing solutions good enough to solve their problem/meet their needs or desires?**	*That the existing ways to sell could be improved upon*
Section C: **Are they prepared to take the necessary actions to get another solution?**	*1) Prepared to invest time & money into a new sales opportunity* *2) Prepared for continual changing environment, trial & error*
Section D: (Optional) **How do they feel about your idea?**	*1) Shop units are appealing* *2) Terms, conditions & costs are acceptable*

Try it for yourself!

- -

Remember you can download the template from productdoctor.co.uk

TOP TIPS

Take this opportunity to tackle those elements of your hypothesis that make you most nervous!

Use the four main sections of risk as shortcut and checklist for your riskiest assumptions

Enter your risky assumptions into the CORE template so you can easily move onto create corresponding questions in the next step

COMMON PITFALLS

Prioritising risky assumptions related to solutions rather than first focusing on customer and user problems, needs and desires

Carrying out unnecessary research where evidence already exists

Obsessing about delivery related risks when you don't yet know what it is you need to build!

STEP 3

CREATE QUESTIONS

KEY POINTS

- Create questions that get evidence for the risky assumptions you have identified
- Write questions in a way that gets honest, relevant and rich answers from your interviewees
- See the dos and don'ts of using materials in the interview

You are arriving at this step with your hypothesis from Step 1 (Write hypothesis) and a list of your riskiest assumptions from Step 2 (Identify risks). In this step you are writing the questions to ask interviewees in Step 6 (Conduct interviews).

These questions are crafted to get evidence to address those risky assumptions. There are lots of tips in this step to help you write questions to access honest, rich and useful insight.

Remember that nothing is set in stone. Your idea may be changing as you move through these steps so if you are changing your mind about anything, you can always go back and make changes to Step 1 (Write hypothesis) and Step 2 (Identify risks). This whole process is flexible and it is entirely expected that you will need to go back and forward while you are working on the idea, so there is no need to get stuck!

How to write good questions

Before we start, let's give a little thought to how to ask questions that prompt an interviewee to talk openly and honestly and without you influencing their answers.

Using open and closed questions

Closed questions are those which can be answered by a simple 'yes' or 'no,' and maybe a 'maybe'! Open-ended questions are those which require more than a simple one-word answer. Both have their place.

Closed questions can be used to establish facts. They can help you to decide whether there are further questions you want to ask, so a closed question can be followed by an open question as shown here:

Did you enjoy reading this book? (closed question: yes, no, possibly a middle ground 'I quite enjoyed it' answer)

What was it about it that you liked / did not like? (open question)

Open questions will get you more information as they prompt fuller answers. So, when you are trying to get information from an interviewee, you should design more open questions like these:

Tell me about other books you have read that you enjoyed. . .

What puts you off reading a book?

When do you tend to read?

Avoid leading questions

What do you like about this book? This is a leading question that assumes that they like something about the book. You may be subconsciously or perhaps overtly trying to get them to answer a question in a particular way. Either way, it leads the interviewee. Instead, you can ask something like *Is there anything you like about this book?* It is particularly important to avoid leading questions when you are trying to establish that the problem exists. Can you get them to tell you that it is a problem rather than you suggesting to them that it's a problem? So, for example, you are interviewing a parent and you want them to tell you that they cannot get on with their chores because little Billy is demanding attention. Your line of questioning will ask them to talk to you about the last time they were doing a chore while in charge of little Billy. If you do not detect any frustration, you ask them about the time before that and then the time before that. If there is any pain there, it will come out.

Avoid hypotheticals

If we put these features into this app would you download it? What people say and what they do are totally different. Instead, you will dig for real evidence of them having done something similar, to draw a parallel. *When did you last do that?* is a good question to start the interviewee talking about a real example. Ground your conversations in real examples.

Simple questions generate clearer answers

If you ask complicated questions, they will be difficult to answer as the interviewee will have to work out what you are trying to ask before they can answer it! This will generate complicated answers that you will then need to clarify and break down further, wasting time and energy. For example, avoid asking multiple questions as one question, for example *How did you feel and what did you do?* It is easier to answer if you split them into two questions. Use plain language, so rather than ask *What is your strategy for dealing with this eventuality?* you can just ask *What did you do when that happened?*

Write your big questions first

For the purposes of writing the research questions and completing this step, it is best to focus on the big questions first. Think of these questions as a funnel, where you start more broadly and then get more specific based on the answers you get. You may see that some big questions in my examples are closed, soliciting just a yes or no answer. When you actually carry out the interview, you will add in follow-up questions to dig out all the information you need based on the answers you get. At this stage, I am not going to write down all the follow-up question possibilities as I want to keep it simple and make sure that the most important areas are covered. You will not be able to predict these follow-up questions as they will be a spur-of-the-moment response to what your interviewees say. We will discuss how to follow up on those questions and dig more in Step 6 (Conduct interviews) when we actually carry out the research.

Ten is a good number

Try to keep within a maximum of ten big questions overall. This does not include all the follow-up questions you will add in during the conversation. If you find that you have more than ten, then either:

- Your value proposition and hypothesis are too complicated and will not all fit into one research interview or

- Your questions go too far beyond just the value proposition and hypothesis or

- You have gone beyond the main ten and are counting all the follow-up questions too or

- You have too many questions for one research session, so prioritise your top questions and then if need be, hold another round of research. You will probably find that your second round will be far more focused and may even have taken you off in a different direction as you will have learned a lot from your first.

Questions respond to the four risk categories

Here is a set of questions, using the indoor market project as an example, where the group being interviewed are potential test traders. It is important to write different sets of questions for each of the different groups of people (think back to the 'people map'). You may find that they are similar to each other, but they are likely to need some fine tuning to suit the different groups.

Example: Questions to address each risk category in the indoor market project

Interview section	Risky assumption	Interview questions
Section A: Does the problem, need or desire exist?	That they want a longer term retail space to sell their offering	Where have you sold your <offering> in the past? Have you rented or considered renting retail premises? Are there any other sales opportunities that you have considered or are considering? What interests you about this particular opportunity?
Section B: Are the existing solutions good enough to solve their problem/meet their needs or desires?	That the existing ways to sell could be improved upon (that there is room for another or new way to sell)	Thinking about where you can sell today (a) What appeals about each opportunity? (b) Is there anything that concerns you? (c) Describe your ideal trading opportunity. . .

Interview section	Risky assumption	Interview questions
Section C: Are they prepared to take the necessary actions to get another solution?	1) Prepared to invest time and money into a new sales opportunity 2) Prepared for continual changing environment, trial and error	Can you give me any examples of where you invested time and money to make some sales? Do you have an example of when you were one of the first to try out a new sales opportunity? Given what you know about this potential opportunity, are you prepared to invest time and a little money to get yourself set up as a trader? How do you feel about working within this new project where there is going to be a period of trial and error for everyone?
Section D: (Optional) How do they feel about your idea?	1) Shop units are appealing	Let's go into the market and look at the empty shop units. (a) Are there particular shop unit(s) that appeal to you? (b) Do you have any questions? (c) Do you have any suggestions?
	2) Terms, conditions and costs are acceptable	Here is some draft paperwork (a) Is there anything that you are pleased to see? (b) Do you have any concerns or questions? (c) Are there any changes you would propose?

You will see that the four risk categories have now become the four interview question sections, A to D. Here are tips on how to write questions in each of these categories:

Section A question tips

Does the problem, need or desire exist? As you will see in the above example, the first set of questions are around whether the problem, need or desire exists as you envisage it. The potential test trader interviewee is being quizzed on where they have sold their product/service to date and whether they have ever sold through or considered a retail opportunity. They are also being asked what appeals about each particular opportunity. All these questions will unlock information around the first part of the value proposition statement which is about who the proposition is for and what needs/desires they have.

They also help you to understand how big the problem, need and desire is, which is really important to establish. You need to know whether it is big enough for them to do anything about.

To avoid getting into hypotheticals and to make this whole conversation as real as you can, use these first questions to get the interviewee to start giving you real examples and stories about their recent experiences. You can continue to refer to them in the rest of the interview.

Try to write questions that get the interviewee to tell you the story of what happened, rather than just a straightforward account. If you can encourage them into storyteller mode with the questions that you ask, then they will become more animated in their responses and you will get greater insight of their feelings.

Here are some other examples that may help you to craft your own questions: In the taxi app example, you might ask:

Have you ever had a poor experience from a taxi company?

When did that last happen?

Can you tell me about what happened?

Do you have any other examples you can tell me about?

Again, using these types of example-based questions, you are getting them to start to tell you the story and you will be able to assess whether it is a problem or need from the way they talk about it, and you will get a good sense of how great that problem or need is.

Another good tip is to try and get them to tell you what the problem, need or desire is rather than you telling them. The issue with you telling them, is that you may be leading them to an answer that you want to hear. It might be that the problem you have identified is not as big as other problems they have. If you ask a suitably open question, like this one about the poor experiences they have had in general then you will hear whether your problem features and if so, whether it is one of the most important ones or not. Of course, if they reel off lots of problems, you can ask them to prioritise the problems that they have listed.

It is a bit of an art to get them to tell you what the problem is and you will get better at this over time.

Later on, as you get ready to carry out the research in Step 6 (Conduct interviews), you will need to work out how long to spend on each section. This is a classic place where interviewers over run as they probe to get the interviewee to tell them what the problem is. They find the interview time has gone and they are still in section A!

Section B question tips

Are the existing solutions good enough to solve their problem/ meet their needs or desires? Now you've explored the existence and had some indication of the level of the problem, need or desire, you can move into what they did to solve it and how well that solution served them. Now it may be that they used a pre-made solution, or maybe they cobbled together their own solution. It is also possible that they did nothing at all and just suffered. Whatever the answer is, you need to write questions that delve into how well that worked for them. By doing this you will get more information about whether there is room for another solution. If they are not totally satisfied with today's solutions, then there is an opportunity for you to give them something better. If they had no solution and just suffered, it is not a given that there is an opportunity for you. The opportunity only exists if the pain, or desire, associated with having no solution is big enough for them to do something about.

In the above indoor market, potential test traders example, you will see that the questions are going to get them to talk about other sales experiences. If they have no previous experiences and have never looked for premises before then you will not be able to pursue this line of questioning, so instead you could try to uncover any previous thoughts and feelings that they have by asking something like *Why have you not looked for premises to date?* That will help you to see their desire and give you a gauge of how strong their desire is. You will also hear all about their concerns which is part of your assessment about current solutions.

By talking through what they did, or thought about doing, you will also get information about your competitors. Remember here that 'competitors' is used in a broad sense as discussed in Step 1 (Write hypothesis), in the 'unlike' section on value proposition statements. Whatever they did to address the problem is your competitor – even if they did nothing!

Here are some generic questions you can use here in section B. They have just told you about a problem, need or desire, so these questions will help you find out whether the current solutions on offer are up to scratch:

You just told me about … So, what did you do?

   (a) Is there anything that is working out well for you?

   (b) Is there anything that is not working so well?

   (c) Is there anything you wish you had been offered?

Through these answers, you should also get some help on what your category of product is. Listen carefully to how the interviewee describes their solution as they may tell you what category their solution was in. You should hear about the job that it is doing for them, which may change the category of product that you wrote in your value proposition statement. For example, thinking about a gaming app for children, this could be in the category of 'things to occupy your child while you need to do something else' rather than just the category of being an app.

If you are concerned about the interviewee's ability to recall what they did to the level of detail that you want, or about whether you will be able to imagine what they describe, then you can ask them to do some preparation before the research interview. If it is appropriate, you can ask them to bring information about the existing solutions they use; for example, if you are looking into online learning products, you can ask an interviewee to bring a list of current websites and apps that they use; or you can ask potential market traders to bring any photographs of stalls or shops where they have sold their products before and so on. Maybe it is relevant for them to keep a diary over the past week that they bring with them and talk through at this point.

The Trilogy: the gift that keeps on giving

'The Trilogy' is the name I have given to a three-question structure that I use all the time. The three fundamental elements are designed to get the interviewee to tell you

(a) *if there is anything they think is positive*

(b) *if there is anything they think is negative and*

(c) *if there is any improvement they can suggest.*

It is a format that you can use throughout customer interviews when you want an interviewee to review something that has happened, or something they have seen. The Trilogy works in various guises and the phrasing can be tweaked to work in different ways depending on what you want reviewed.

These three very efficient questions will help you get the interviewee to carry out an active assessment in front of you and will tease out some very important insight. They are a set of questions to help you to get the most information you can. You may script them in as your main questions (as you can see in the examples given) as well as a set of questions that you can use to dig deeper once you are in the actual conversation.

Let's imagine that they have just told you about what they did to solve a particular problem or meet a need or desire. Here is where the trilogy comes into play. You can ask them

(a) *Is there anything that worked well for you / Is there anything you like about it?*

(b) *Is there anything that did not work well for you / Is there anything that you don't like about it?*

(c) *Is there anything you would improve about that experience / Is there anything you wish you had?*

Using these questions will get you a review of current solutions. It will also reveal any ideas they may have had about solving the problem where they might have thought 'If only I had been offered . . .'.

You may notice that I ask *Is there anything that works well?* rather than *What works well?* This is to avoid leading the interviewee. If you ask *What went well?* it is assuming that there is something that went well, whereas if you ask *Is there anything that went well?* you are not pushing them to find something that went well if they did not really think that there was anything positive.

You can run The Trilogy questions every time you are given an example of a solution that the interviewee has used. It is a great way to probe further when you are talking about real experiences.

Section C question tips

Are they prepared to take the necessary actions to get another solution? This section is going to help you with your risky assumptions around the action that you need the interviewee to take so that you can reach your goal. You need to ask the interviewee to give you examples of when they have taken the sorts of actions you are looking for them to take. This will give you evidence that they would be prepared to take the actions you need them to. In some cases that is easy, for example with the indoor market project, you can ask the potential test traders whether they have spent any money on a sales opportunity before, or taken a gamble and tried out a sales opportunity in an unknown environment. If the actions you need them to take feel very new, then you can try to find a parallel situation. For example, if you are looking to be the first-to-market with a taxi app, you will not be able to get evidence that they have paid for taxis using their mobile before. However, you can ask them about other things that they have paid for using their mobile. Dig into those examples and try to find real incidents where it was efficient for them to make payments from their mobile. And there is your evidence! Of course, there are all sorts of other actions, such as whether they would be prepared to download something or plug something into their existing gadget, or consider an alternative way to do something, or change suppliers and so on.

If they did adopt a solution from a third party, get them to tell you the story of how they came to adopt it as this will generate insight around how you can attract your future customer and/or users. How did they know that the solution existed? Can they talk to you through the signup process? These sorts of questions will give you more understanding about your target customer and what job they are trying to get done.

Here are some example questions for this section:

Tell me how the final decision was made about the option you chose?

How much did it cost?

Have you ever spent any money on anything else like this before?

By asking these questions, you should be able to discover whether there were any influencers (think back to the 'people map'). You may also find that someone else paid, which means that the person you think is your customer may actually be your user.

By answering this last question, (whether they have spent money on anything like this before), you will discover which category they put your idea into. Think back to the value proposition statement where you reference which 'category' you are in. Note that your customer and/or user may have just told you which category they see you in and potentially which job you can help them to get done. They are telling you the benefit you can bring them, so listen carefully!

More example questions for this section are:

Are there other <insert broad things like this> that you have paid for over the past year?

Can you tell me the last time you needed to use it?

<Enter. . . The Trilogy>

    (a) *Was there anything that worked particularly well for you?*

    (b) *Was there anything that did not work particularly well for you?*

    (c) *Is there anything you would improve about that experience / What do you wish it would have done for you?*

If you have had information from previous sections, you can frame the question this way:

You have talked about what you did – now I am interested in how you made the decision to do that. . .

    How did you know that solution was available?

    Did you consider any other options?

    Why did you choose this over other options?

    Can you talk me through how you signed up?

There is also an opportunity to add The Trilogy questions to find out what they liked about the process, did not like and would improve.

Section D question tips

How do they feel about your idea? Do you have an early design, a prototype, a beta, a half or fully complete solution? Well here is your opportunity to add in a section D. I know that some of you will be trying to find a business model for something you have already designed, built or thought through. Well if you have, and if there is time, you have a chance to open your kimono and give your interviewees a sneak preview!

You can do this only if you have exhausted questions around the value proposition and hypothesis and there is genuinely time left in the interview. If you move onto this section too quickly then you may not have fully understood what the customer and/ or user needs and we know where that ends up – a solution that is not wanted. We need to find out everything about what they are doing and how they are feeling first before we share any of our ideas. Talking about solutions any earlier can cloud and bias their answers. I know how enticing it is to share a solution idea and I know that innovators cannot get there fast enough, but please be disciplined. I add this fourth section in as I understand the passion, but it must not be abused! So please, no rushing through the first three sections to get to this fourth.

If you do not have any ideas about your solution then please do stay that way. Don't force it. But if you have some early ideas, you certainly can bring them out of the cupboard right now!

If you have an interviewee who has not answered positively to previous questions, you could still show them your potential solution as they may have interesting insight to give you.

Here are some example questions that work well in section D:

Have you seen anything else like this? This will flush out competitors that you may not have thought of and other offerings that you would not have thought were anything to do with your offering!

How would you describe this to someone else? This is a brilliant question to get them to articulate the benefits in their own words.

Then you can add that straight back into the next iteration of your value proposition

Does this feel like something you would like? This question goes straight for the jugular. Observe body language carefully on this one as you may see a squirm which somewhat negates a positive answer.

I have been very surprised at the answers to this. I would have sworn that an interviewee did not like a solution but overall, they definitely thought it was for them and the opposite has also happened. So I would definitely ask this question if you are showing something.

Using materials in section D

If you have nothing to actually show, but you have a concept that you want to describe, you could use a written piece. The interviewee is often going to grasp it better if they see something, even if it is just written, rather than if you sit there and just describe it.

You could also show the material as a build, showing first just a paragraph of the overall description and then you could show a three or four page description giving more information, stopping after each of the two pieces to ask your Trilogy questions:

(a) *Is there anything in particular that you like about this?*

(b) *Do you have any questions?*

(c) *What do you hope that it will do?*

Question (b) will tease out things that they don't like about it without suggesting to them that there are things they may not like.

You might like to use a storyboard. It is a drawing that shows the interviewee in a scenario and what they are going to experience, a bit like a comic strip. Showing a customer and/or user featuring in the storyboard can really help to better explain the experience you are trying to create as it puts the interviewee visually into the scenario.

Again, as it is pre-prepared material, it goes some way to helping you to create a consistent experience across numerous interviews.

In the indoor market project example, at this point in the conversation, we walk into the market and show the actual empty shop units. The ultimate material for some research will be like this, in situ, as the materials will be all around you. In this project, the conversation with potential test traders happened at a coffee shop near the market and then we moved into the market itself. Otherwise, you may have materials that you want to create to do this job of making your solution very real.

Avoid overloading the interviewee

I recommend that you 'drip feed' the description of the solution so you don't overload the interviewee. You do not want them to feel bombarded. Remember that this will be the first time they see an idea of your solution and it may take a while for them to take it all in. Whatever material you use, including just describing it there and then, it is best to try to keep your descriptions to less than three minutes. Videos are best at less than three or four minutes. I have used videos for up to seven minutes and that felt too long. If you find your materials are much longer, then you can take a break halfway through and ask relevant questions. The Trilogy format works well here too.

Competitors can provide great materials

It is a good idea to use material to bring a concept to life even if it is not created by you. If there is already a product, service or offering on the market that has some or all of the elements that you are considering, then you can use that as material in your research too. This will save you loads of time! You can also think about adding annotations to paper versions of other products so you can better explain what you are thinking.

Pre-recording to keep consistency

I am a big fan of using pre-recorded descriptions so that what you show and the way you show it is consistent throughout all the interviews. So if you have something to show, for example a mock up on your computer, then you can make a video of yourself talking over it. There are plenty of free video tools you can use as well as taking video from your mobile.

Sharing the value proposition statement

I have shared printed out value proposition statements in research sessions and asked for interviewees to critique what is written there. This works really well as a structure. The interviewee will tell you whether they agree with pain points or desires you have identified, whether you have understood the situation in which they experience the pain or desire, whether you have understood the benefits properly and whether you have identified the competition as they see it. You can see all the areas of conversation this can spark, and it also works as a nice checkpoint for the first few interview sections. There is no harm asking a question a number of different ways to see if you can get at more information each time and as a way to check that you have heard the answer correctly.

In the story below I explain how I shared value proposition statements in interviews and had the interviewees help me rewrite them so that they were truly reflective of how they felt as potential customers. The project was to establish the branding and positioning for a new business consultancy.

Story: Asking interviewees to write a value proposition statement to create a brand for a new mobile telecoms consultancy

My interviewees were all very senior directors of businesses who use consultancies with particular expertise around different aspects of mobile telecommunications. I gave them the value proposition statement printed out on a sheet of paper with a red pen and asked them to go through each element, starting with 'FOR (Who has the need or desire?)', just as we did in Step 1 (Write hypothesis). I asked them to critique and suggest rewrites to make it truly reflective for them as they were the 'FOR' in this instance. In doing so, I understood more about how they felt, what they needed and how this new consultancy could improve upon the service they were getting from other consultants. For example, we discovered that these business clients are very wary of consultants getting a foot in the door who try to stay for as long as possible; that they are miffed when the sale is made to them by a senior person with experience and then an inexperienced consultant is sent to do the work and that they value consultants who have 'been there and done that'.

Avoid getting into conversations about branding or features

If you are showing some material, it is best to leave off product names and/or branding. If it is there, then it will be a distraction and now is not the time to get into that discussion! Try to focus on the benefits that you can deliver them first rather than get into feedback around the product name or visual brand. If your imagined idea does not resonate that it doesn't matter what you call it, what whizz and bang features you are going to add or how you are going to brand it.

Avoid conducting a usability test!

A usability test is where you have an interface and you want to find out whether it is easy to use, whether it is intuitive enough for the user to get from A to B. But it is way too early for that in the idea test! So, if you show them a working prototype, remember that just as you are not there to test branding or the detail of features, you are also not there to test whether it works as they would expect it would.

Even if you have a prototype you may decide not to show it so that you avoid falling into this trap. I have been in the situation a number of times and recommended that we keep the prototype away from the interviewee at this stage to avoid getting into the usability conversation as we really needed to focus on their needs and desires first. You can always just show a description of your intended solution with an explanation that shows how you are going to deliver the benefits that respond to their problems, needs and desires that you have identified.

Using materials in a video call

When I use materials in a physical interview, I tend to use printed out material and give the interviewee a pen to scribble their notes straight on to the material. If I have something to show them on the screen, such as a video or a mocked up website page, then I just turn around my laptop so they can see it.

If I am on a video call, I share a document online with them, send the link in the video call chat box and give them edit rights. So those who want to can make notes directly on to the document. Where relevant, I also show material by just sharing my screen, making sure that I can still see their face to gauge their response.

Completing The Really Good Idea Test templates

- -

Are you working on your own idea as you go through this book?

If so, then you should still be using the CORE template. Remember that you can download these templates from productdoctor.co.uk.

You are now ready to complete the highlighted boxes for Step 3 (Create questions).

You can see that Step 1 (Write hypothesis) and Step 2 (Risky assumptions) are shaded as you will have completed them, as are the steps that you have not reached yet, Step 4 (Find interviewees) and Step 5 (Measures and targets).

THE REALLY GOOD IDEA TEST **CORE**		❸ CREATE QUESTIONS
Section A: Does the problem, need or desire exist?		
Section B: Are the existing solutions good enough to solve their problem/meet their needs or desires?		*Enter Step 3's Questions*
Section C: Are they prepared to take the necessary actions to get another solution?		
Section D: (Optional) How do they feel about your idea?		

What do I write in this box?

Add the relevant questions against the relevant risks that you completed in Step 2 (Identify risks). Here is example of questions for the potential test traders in our example from the indoor market project. I have left in the Step 2 Risks so you can see how the questions correspond to them.

② IDENTIFY RISKS	③ CREATE QUESTIONS
That they want a longer term retail space to sell their offering	Where have you sold your <offering> in the past? Have you rented or considered renting retail premises? Are there any other sales opportunities that you have considered or are considering? What interests you about this particular opportunity?
That the existing ways to sell could be improved upon	Thinking about where you can sell today (a) What appeals about each opportunity? (b) Is there anything that concerns you? (c) Describe your ideal trading opportunity...
1) Prepared to invest time & money into a new sales opportunity 2) Prepared for continual changing environment, trial & error	1) Can you give me any examples of where you invested time and money to make some sales? Do you have an example of when you were one of the first to try out a new sales opportunity? 2) Given what you know about this potential opportunity, are you prepared to invest time and a little money to get yourself set up as a trader? How do you feel about working within this new project where there is going to be a period of trial and error for everyone?
1) Shop units are appealing 2) Terms, conditions & costs are acceptable	1) Let's go into the market and look at the empty shop units. (a) Are there particular shop unit(s) that appeal to you? (b) Do you have any questions? (c) Do you have any suggestions? 2) Take a look at this draft paperwork (a) Is there anything that you are pleased to see? (b) Do you have any concerns or questions? (c) Are there any changes you would propose?

Try it for yourself!

- -

Remember you can download the templates from productdoctor.co.uk.

TOP TIPS

Construct simple questions: Complicated questions will get you complicated answers!

See if you can create questions that get them to tell you that they have a problem or need rather than you telling them

Use 'The Trilogy' question format when an opportunity to delve further arises

COMMON PITFALLS

Failing to pay attention to all four interview sections and going straight to testing the solution (in section D)

Writing hypothetical questions that will waste time on hypothetical answers

Cramming too much into the interview

STEP ④

FIND INTERVIEWEES

KEY POINTS

Write recruitment criteria for your interviewees

Get the right 'mix' of interviewees

See how to do the recruitment yourself

Thanks to Step 3 (Create questions) you now know what to ask to unlock the evidence you need to address those risky assumptions you identified in Step 2 (Identify risks). In this step we work on identifying your ideal customer and/or user groups and creating a list of recruitment criteria. Think of this as a shopping list of the basics that you need. You will already have started thinking about these criteria right back in Step 1 (Write hypothesis) when you thought through the people who will benefit from your idea in the value proposition statements.

To generate your recruitment criteria, you will look at 'demographic' and then 'situational' elements. The demographics will help you work out characteristics such as age, gender, location and the situational elements will be about the backdrop and conditions that put them in the position of needing, wanting or desiring a solution. These will become fixed criteria that each interviewee has to meet. Then, you need to set out the 'mix' that you want to find so that you have diversity within the group and it is not too homogenous. You might like to think of the mix as the variable elements to ensure that, for example, they are not all male, or are not all twenty to thirty years old, unless your recruitment criteria demand that. Together, the recruitment criteria and mix make up your 'group profile'.

You need to find only five interviewees for a group profile to start with. In this step we will look at how to find them. You can also consider if you want to find an additional sixth person to act as a wildcard as this will help to test out assumptions that you may not realise you have made.

Why face-to-face research is so important

Before we go any further, I need to stop you from making a very common mistake. Almost without fail, every innovator that I talk with wants to jump straight to doing a survey at this early stage. When I ask them why, they say that it is quick to build and easy to put out on social media. They also say that they will be able to reach large numbers of people. When I dig a little deeper, I also find out that they would prefer to hide behind their screens rather than get in front of customers and users! It's a modern phenomenon.

As well as meeting interviewees in person, carrying out interviews over video are a very valid way to carry out face to face research.

Here are the arguments for carrying out face-to-face research rather than doing a survey:

Face-to-face means you can see emotion. We are doing this research to try and uncover underlying reasons, opinions and motivations. You need to get answers to 'how' and 'why' type questions. The evidence you are trying to find is all about satisfying needs and desires, exploring pain and how you can provide relief. That is emotional. How can you possibly analyse emotion through a survey? You need to see your interviewees' eyes to feel their emotions, see the pain, feel the desire so that you can understand their motivations. On a survey you can't hear what they are thinking as they take a moment to answer a survey question and you can't see their expressions when they tick a box.

Face-to-face offers you so much more through nonverbal communication; from body language, facial expressions and intonation. There are a lot of studies that show well over 50 per cent of communication comes from body language and more than 30 per cent from tone of voice. Mehrabian's study in 1967 is often cited: Words only account for 7 per cent, tone of voice is 38 per cent and body language is the all-important one at 55 per cent.

Face-to-face means that you can easily probe to get deeper insight. When you are in front of an interviewee, there is the opportunity to pick up on clues that there is more information they may be able to give you. You do not get that chance in a survey. So, for example, you can say *I see that you hesitated over that answer – why was that?* or *You sounded frustrated then – did I get that right? Why was that?* You get so much more understanding when you can spot these clues and probe further.

Face-to-face means that you can show stuff to each other! In interview section B, which is the second of the four interview sections shown in Step 3 (Create questions) and shown on the CORE template, you will be looking into what interviewees currently do to resolve the problem, meet their needs or satisfy their desire. If you are face-to-face, then an interviewee can show you what they are employing to do that job today. You will also be able to share any materials you are using more easily.

If it is totally impractical to organise a face-to-face interview, then try to do a video call as at least you will still be able to pick up on body language and intonation and failing that, use the telephone.

One-to-one interviews, pairs or groups?

If it is particularly fundamental to the proposition, it can really be good to interview in pairs or groups. I have done this for new person-to-person messaging ideas and two-player gaming products, where I recruited two users who were friends. Being able to hear a discussion between two friends will bring you even richer insight as they are naturally more open in their conversation. Having discovered that students often study in pairs, I have also carried out interviews for revision products with friends who study together. If you are thinking about a new product, feature or service that is going to be consumed by groups of people together, then it may also make sense to run a group session. For example, a multiplayer game, work team, sport or social activity.

I do run group research sessions for early-stage value proposition testing if I think that talking as a group is going to give me a lot of additional insight versus one-to-one interviews. If you are working on an experience that will be enjoyed in a group, it certainly makes sense to carry out research in groups later down the line, where you have something to show. So when you have a prototype or early version of the product, you will want to test it out with the group all at the same time.

If the subject is emotive, it is better to avoid groups as people would find that too exposing and may not like to share emotions in a group environment. Peer pressure also can be immense. For example, I hate paint-balling but do not want to appear to be a party pooper in front of my work team! You may think that talking about a new range of Christmas products is not emotional, but think about how much pressure people feel around creating a good Christmas for their families and about dealing with in-laws and getting the turkey cooked right and . . . melt down!!

I would not recommend you run group research unless you are very experienced as the logistics are more complicated and you need to manage the actual conversation far more closely. Running group sessions requires more coordination as you need to try and get all your interviewees to turn up at the same time and more effort to find a suitable quiet and private space to carry out the research sessions. Of course you can use online group video calling functionality as long as your connection is good and location is peaceful. You also need to be practised in keeping all interviewees engaged and managing the dynamics of different personalities in the group discussion to ensure that everyone has the opportunity to speak. If you are a novice and you really feel that a group discussion is crucial, then you could always find someone more experienced to help you.

Writing your recruitment criteria

Demographic factors

Let's start creating our shopping list of recruitment criteria. Below you will see a list of demographic factors. Consider these as a starting point to profile your ideal customers and/or users. Throughout this activity, it is useful to think about completing the following statement 'It is pointless to interview them unless they. . . '.

Demographics	Examples
Job status, sector, job title, certification?	Construction, part-time, site manager, 'Master Builder'. . .
Nationality / Ethnicity / Residency	UK resident / For how many years . . .
Languages spoken?	Fluent English speaker
Age?	Fifteen to twenty years old

Demographics	Examples
Gender?	Female, male, other, prefer not to say. . .
Education level?	University, School . . .
Where do they live?	Rural, town, near a river, in a flat, second property. . .
Financial status?	Low, medium, high income, mortgage, loans . . . .
Marital status / family set up?	Single parent, two kids under the age of ten. . .
Write your own!	*What criteria are particularly relevant for your opportunity?*

Regarding the demographic around languages spoken, you may like to find out whether they are able to hold a good conversation. I heard a great story from another researcher about a group of interviewees that were recruited through a university professor; unfortunately, the group were all foreign students and their English was very limited. That seriously hindered the research as they did not speak the same language. Often agencies who handle recruitment will have a phone conversation with each potential interviewee as they confirm arrangements and that is the way that they check whether the person is chatty enough to be a good candidate. If you do not do this, then you will need to add 'fluent in <enter particular language>' into your recruitment criteria.

If your customer is a business, these demographics may be more appropriate:

Demographics	Examples
What sector?	Health, Retail, Transport, Education . . .
What profession?	Accountant, engineer . . .
Company status?	Limited company, sole trader, partnership . . .

Demographics	Examples
Company size?	One to ten employees, eleven to a hundred employees . . .
Financial status?	Not yet profitable, one to two million pounds profit per annum . . .
Composition of company?	Number of employees, years trading, have a Sales Director . . .
Where are they based?	Multi-site/single site location, urban, rural, coastal . . .
Their customer base?	Stay-at-home dads, universities, restaurants . . .
Write your own!	*What criteria are particularly relevant for your opportunity?*

You can add demographic criteria both positively, for example, they need to be between twenty to thirty years old and negatively. For example, in previous research projects, I have excluded teachers from research with parents about their children's education as they are likely to not be representative of a standard parent as they are too close to the education system themselves. I have excluded people who work in marketing from research about how best to position a product designed to meet their particular needs as it would be difficult for them to give their personal rather than professional opinion. I have also excluded journalists and business bloggers from new ideas that my client would not want to see plastered over the morning press!

When deciding on your demographics, you may also want to ask yourself to complete this statement 'I do not want them if they. . .'.

Situational elements

Next you need to add to the list those situational elements that put them into your ideal customer and/or user group. What is the relevant situation, backdrop, conditions that put them there?

Here is a story to explain why it is important to really think through the situational elements so that you do not waste your time interviewing the wrong people.

Story: Recruited interviewees had no intention of ever paying to listen to music on their mobile

It was the early days of apps and I carried out some research groups with young teens about a new mobile music app. They loved it and made some amazing suggestions about what it should do. I moved onto talking with them about price, asking them what mobile stuff and music they had spent money on. They told me that they never paid for music or apps at all and never intended to. In fact, as their phones were on their parent's account, they would be asking them to pay and music was not something their parents would ever be prepared to fund. The point of this story is that to avoid wasting time, the selection criteria could have included that the young teens needed to have spent money on an app or on music before. It would have avoided wasting time in these research conversations

Based on questions written in Step 3 (Create questions), think about what minimum criteria you want to add to identify your ideal customer and/or user group. Try completing this statement: 'It is pointless to interview them unless they. . . '.

Here is a list of considerations for thinking through the situational elements:

Frequency – do they do it often enough to be in our ideal customer and/or user group? Using the taxi app as an example, you will want to find people who take a taxi often enough to care. If they do not, then may not feel the pain frequently enough to do anything about it. Of course, there are things that people will do once a year that are important enough and painful enough like cooking a Christmas dinner, or doing a tax return. In these cases, an annual frequency would be enough.

Recentness – is their experience current enough? (Yes that is a word, I looked it up!) Is their experience current enough for them to be able to remember the scenario clearly enough to give us useful information? Emotions can fade over time. So if, for example, you are carrying out some research with students about taking exams, then it is best to interview them just after they have done that. In this case, you may build a time restriction into your recruitment criteria; that they have done this thing within the past week, month or year. You could of course have both frequency and recentness; that someone does it more than once a month and the last time they did it was within the past month.

Familiarity – have they done it before? Think about the part of our hypothesis that sets out what we will need people to do to get the benefit we are offering. Are we asking them to do something they have never done before? Will they need persuading or educating to engage with our idea on a basic level? If so, then question whether they should be in our ideal group. Here is the story of how I learned the lesson about familiarity:

Story: Researching an iPad app with non-iPad using teachers

In the early days of iPads, I ran a research group with some teachers. The intention was to find out if they were open to incorporating digital learning delivered via the iPad into their lessons. The interviewees were not iPad users so I spent the whole session trying to sell in the benefits of using an iPad, rather than having the conversation I needed to have!

So there is little point identifying someone who has not already adopted a new way of doing things if that behaviour is fundamental to your offering. Your offering will feel ahead of its time and they would not be ready for it yet. So, for example, if you are looking at developing a new app, where you will want people to pay via the app as that is fundamental to your business model, you had better make sure that you include in your recruitment criteria that they use apps and make payments through apps! There are some people that are still very averse to paying for anything through their mobile and if that is fundamental to what you need them to do, then you do not want them in your ideal group. Here is another story that brings this point life.

Story: Researching smartphone-based learning with students who find their mobile too distracting when studying

I was running some research around ways for students to revise. The learning services were all based around students using their mobile phones. During the research I discovered that around half of the students in the particular group physically put their mobiles away when they are sitting down to study. They said that they found their mobiles far too distracting and they could too easily start messaging friends or surfing the internet (I'm sure we can all relate!).

Parallels – can you find something similar? If you cannot find any points of familiarity, you need to think a bit more laterally. Can you find some kind of parallel situation? You want to find out if a parent would pay for an app to entertain their child while they are getting on with their necessary chores. So, you really want to find out if the parent is prepared to pay for something that will keep their child busy for an hour. That would give you some evidence that they are prepared to pay to get that job done. You probably would also want to find a parent who had in the past paid for an app as some people, on principle, say that they will never pay for an app. So they may not have paid for an app to entertain their kid, but they have paid for some other apps before.

Considered solutions – have they tried to find an alternative?
Has your ideal interviewee thought about or done anything
about finding an alternative? If they have, then that would show
that their need, problem or desire is big enough to do something
about. So in our indoor market project example, if the potential
test traders have tried getting some kind of retail space before,
even just at a school fete, then it shows their appetite, otherwise
they might not be committed or interested enough in this new
opportunity. If you are looking for parents who need something
to keep their children entertained while they get on with chores,
then you need to find parents who have a recent example of trying
to do just that.

Are they serial interviewees? I am afraid that 'serial
interviewees' do exist. They are on the market research trail and
knowing that they can get paid for their input, they apply often
and dare I say, sometimes tell little lies to get in. There are also
people who will not lie, but they do a lot of research. This may or
may not bother you. (Have I said that generally people LOVE to do
research as they get to talk and be listened to!) You can, if you like,
ask a question about how many market research groups they have
done over the past six months, but honestly I am not sure that it is
worth it. I am not too worried about this when I recruit myself, but
if I use an agency to help recruit, I am happy if they want to root
these out.

Creating your 'group profile'

If you are using the templates which are downloadable at product-
doctor.co.uk, you will see that the box for Step 4 (Find interviewees)
asks you to enter your 'group profile'. This is a summary of how
many relevant customers or users you are going to interview, the
main recruitment criteria (they are the fixed demographic and situational element above) and the mix that you are looking for to make
sure that the group is not too homogenous.

Deciding on the size of the group

I have found that five is a good number to start with in a group. While the mix within the group may vary, the recruitment criteria for each of these five people in the group is the same. In my experience, five tends to be the right number to generate enough good initial data. You can always go to more people if you feel after this initial five, that you need more evidence.

You may have started with five from one segment and if you are hearing some consistency, you might want to move to another segment if you feel your mix may be too narrow. See if that remains consistent and if you are hearing more and more consistency, then you are good to go.

If you start to hear very different things, then you may need to go back to Step 1 (Write hypothesis) and review your target customer and/or user value proposition and segments again or perhaps your recruitment criteria needs changing in which case go back to Step 2 (Identify risks).

It is always worth starting small and seeing what happens. You must be disciplined though and go back to previous steps to make changes based on the evidence you get.

It does depend on what you are researching of course, but at this value proposition stage, you could be looking for somewhere between five and twenty total interviews for each specific customer or user segment. Here are some examples of the numbers that I have worked with just to get to the point of being able to say that 'this is a really good idea':

Examples: Number of interviewees and groups across a range of projects

Indoor market project to get empty shop units rented: Five potential renters followed by five potential market visitors

Idea for a new music app for a start-up developer team: Five teenagers

---

New idea for a small business telephone system for a communications company: Five office managers

Developing a virtual world for a social gaming start-up: Two groups of five tweenagers – one in the UK and one in the US

Marketing ideas for mobile operator to stimulate picture messaging: Two groups of five existing mobile operator customers from two distinct customer segments

New revision resources for an education provider: Five students (users) and five parents (customers) in an urban area and five students (users) and five parents (customers) in a rural area

You need to decide what number feels like enough to give you confidence to move forward. Remember that this is just to get you to a point where you can say that you have a really good idea. This will depend on what your idea is and what market you are playing in. That does not mean that you will never talk to a customer or user again, just that it is enough at this stage. For those where I went to more than one group, you can see that either there was a distinct customer and user group, or there were potentially very different profiles within a group, as with the tweenagers (aged between nine and twelve) from the UK being quite different from tweenagers in the US. For more mass market products, like picture messaging, where you are looking at a broad range of mobile phone users, you may like to identify more than one group.

Remember that first off, this is early research to see if your initial value proposition and hypothesis resonate or not. Bit by bit, you can go and get some more evidence once you have built some initial confidence in your idea.

The point is not to worry too much for the time being about what gives you a statistically sound sample. This can be a bit rough and ready right now as you are just trying to work out whether you have an idea that is worth pursuing or not.

Tip: Find a sixth wildcard interviewee

It is very common in the early stages of an idea to put unnecessary limits on the size of your potential customers and/or users without even realising you are doing it. When putting these group profiles together, you are trying to find a bullseye profile. However, this in itself, is full of assumptions. By doing this, you may forget that there could be other groups to go to or worst still, rule them out too early on. Now at this early stage, you do not want to be carrying out too many customer and/or user research interviews, but you do want to avoid this pitfall. So how about you pick one interviewee who you think does not fit your recruitment criteria? Someone outside of your recruitment criteria?

Finding a wildcard can also happen by accident rather than by deliberately recruiting them. You may find that you start interviewing someone who does not fit the profile. If this happens, carry on with the interview as this could be your wildcard! See what you can learn. Then you can recruit someone afterwards to backfill their place in the initial five.

So, interviewing a wildcard will help you to see whether you have a good set of recruitment criteria, whether your hypothesis and underpinning value proposition statements are correct and/or you might learn something that you would not otherwise have found out about. You may even find another group of customers or users to address.

Example: Wildcards showed me that the assumed problem for an online study idea was too narrow

I was interviewing students who could not study the subject they wanted to at school. I found that actually, there are some motivated students who would love to be able to study a subject independently, outside of the 'distracting school environment', regardless of whether their school offered the subject or not. So you can see how the idea of studying a subject online was not going to be just a second-best option responding to that problem, but had a place as a positive choice. This changed the value proposition and broadened the target audience significantly.

Example: Wildcards showed me there was a user and customer for this book

Another example is in relation to this book. I wanted feedback on some visual design options for the book cover. I was only asking people who have read a business-type book over the past two years. As far as I was concerned, they were both my user and my customer. My octogenarian aunt asked me if she could have a look. I told her politely that as she was not the target profile reader of the book so I did not want to be influenced by her view. She explained that she has bought many books of this nature for younger family members and has done so based on the cover design. Obvious, right?! I also chatted to my hairdresser who owns his salon (always a good bet as they can hardly get away from you mid-cut!). I asked him if he read books like this. He said that he did, but never bought any of them for himself. They were given to him as Christmas and birthday gifts.

How many groups to run

Start small. I urge you not to make it too complicated at this stage. Unless you have a customer and user who are different from each other, do not force your interviewees into different group profiles at the start. You can always do this later. For example, let's say you have a broad age range in your potential audience and you anticipate that the younger people think very differently to the older ones, you could run your first set of interviews, making sure that these first recruits represent the mix of ages. Then you can see whether you spotted any differences in their answers. If so, you may then decide to carry out another set of interviews with an older versus a younger age group if it matters for your idea at this early stage.

Put customers and users into different group profiles. You may find that you have groups with different profiles. Each one of these groups will have their own recruitment criteria as they are different. So, for example, if you have customers and users, you should definitely split them into different group profiles. If you have not already realised this in previous steps, you can now split them out and put them through The Really Good Idea Test separately, starting at the beginning with Step 1 (Write hypotheses). There is no problem with going back and running two tracks through the test at the same time or you may like to run one group first through the whole test and then return to the beginning to run the next. Up to you.

Consider what variables make a good mix

You already have the fixed recruitment criteria that each inter-viewee in the group has to meet (other than the wildcard). They are the demographic and situational elements. Outside of those, you need to consider the 'mix' that you want to find so that the group is not too homogenous and 'samey'. For example, unless you are look-ing for a specific gender or age, make sure that you get a good mix across all genders and ages. You might like to think of the mix as the variable element(s) that will make the interviewees different enough to get a good range when you come to recruit. This is particularly important if you have quite a mass market offering. Keep a close eye on this if you are recruiting through your contacts as your circle may be quite homogenous. This is also something you can watch out for while you are recruiting and you adjust this variable once you have confirmed your first few interviewees to get the rest of the mix right.

Finding interviewees who fit your group profile

Using a screener will streamline your recruitment process

A 'screener' is a series of qualifying questions to determine if a person fits specific criteria to participate in a research study. It can be conducted over the phone or online. If online, the screener is usually presented in a survey format. This is where a survey works well! The screener is not there to get insight per se; it is there to help you recruit interviewees who fit your group profile. A screener enables you to capture and give information all in one go, which saves going backwards and forwards with each individual applicant.

There are a range of easily available free survey tools you can use. Do make sure that they work well on mobiles – you don't want to put off potential interviewees who abandon it because of a poor user experience.

Here are the circumstances where you may like to use a screener:

- You have more than a couple of simple recruitment criteria, so in a screener you can ask a (reasonable) number of questions to help you filter out those who fit and do not fit.
- You have additional information to give to help potential interviewees see if they are a fit or not.
- You need to get a good mix and ask those questions.

Resist the temptation of carrying out the whole research in this screener! The purpose of this is to whittle down your list to find the people who fit your criteria, not to start asking your bank of interview questions.

Try also to keep the screener quite short. People do not have much tolerance to answer too many questions. Ten questions feel like too many. You need to also think about how long it takes to complete it. Under five minutes is about right and please do test out how long it takes to complete before putting it live. Even better if you can get someone else to have a go at completing it to check that it flows, makes sense and does not take too long to fill out. There is an example of a screener later in this chapter.

'On the street' recruiting for easy-to-find group profiles

Now you may find that your recruitment criteria are so simple that you can easily find your groups(s) of five just walking down the street! Here are some examples that have worked for me. As you are going into public places and approaching strangers you need to be careful so here is my disclaimer: I accept no responsibility for anything. I am not telling you to do this, I am just giving some examples of what worked for me.

Examples of 'on the street' recruitment

I have done some on-the-spot type of recruitment when I needed to find art students. I printed out some flyers and went down to the college, recruited on the spot and carried out the research there and then in a local cafe.

On another occasion I needed to speak with sixteen-year olds about how they study for exams, so it was down to the local coffee shop when school was finished – I have done this both in the UK and US. In the US, it was an independently owned cafe so I did check with the owner in advance to make sure that they were happy with that and knew what I was doing.

I was running some research to find out the marketing needs and desires of shop owners. I just walked up into my local high street and managed to recruit interviewees who owned the local butcher, estate agent, clothes shop, second-hand record shop and dry cleaners.

In these examples they were new ideas with very simple recruitment criteria.

Reach out to your family, friends and colleagues

If you can recruit yourself, then do. You will learn so much about them through the recruitment process. You will also find that because of this pre-research engagement, interviewees are likely to be more relaxed in the actual research session, which means they will be more open and chatty. You should also save a bit of time when you actually carry out the research as the initial introduction has happened.

Think hard about who you know and who can get you access to. Have you heard about 'six degrees of separation'? It is the idea that all people are six, or fewer, social connections away from each other (originally written about by Frigyes Karinthy, 1929). So you should be able to reach all the people that you need through family, friends, friends of friends and so on.

Email, text, send on messaging services and post on social media to spread the word to your friends and family. Ask them to pass your message on. Social networks are an obvious choice for getting the message out there. I have used professional online social networks to find professional people; local geo-based social networks to find academics and people who wanted to lose weight, my friends' networks for teenagers and the list goes on. Much more is possible than you may think. Think about your business contacts including people you used to work with; people you are connected with in online business networks; go through the business cards you have collected; go to business-related events. I have recruited people through old colleagues, current colleagues; contacting people I knew on LinkedIn and by going to business events.

In your social circles think about your school and college friends, any sports and leisure groups you belong to, community groups, people who you know living and working in your local shops and so on. Family are pretty good to recruit through as they mainly want to help you! Parents, siblings, aunts and uncles, cousins and all the in-laws. Get them to send out your message and have a quick chat to help them work out who they could approach. I have recruited through all my family members at one point or another!

The story below recounts a discussion I had with some PhD students who felt that they were most unconnected as their lives are so focused on research and living and working at a university. It proves my point that most often people do not quite appreciate the reach that they have.

Story: PhD students are way more connected than they think they are!

PhD students at universities are often puzzled about how they are going to get access to the right customers and influencers who might be working at local councils or in large multinationals. They feel quite cut off from the real world. When we start to discuss this, they begin to see that they have a good reach through their university. Universities have rich contact lists through their own innovation programmes, through relationships and collaborations that they have with local businesses. There is a lot that goes on around innovation, employability and graduate recruitment that students aren't aware of so digging around that home territory can be very fruitful. Even where those contacts are not available, I explain that sending an email to the right person saying that you are a PhD student at <this> university in <something very cutting edge and intelligent sounding> will carry weight. Tell them also that you are looking into solving <this particular problem> or have an idea about <x, y and z> and you could well pique the interest of a potential solution-seeking interviewee.

Using one interviewee to find another

In some cases it makes sense to use one interviewee to help you find others as it can save you lots of time in recruitment. This works where one interviewee might have access to more people that look like them; for example, if you are looking for students who are studying a particular subject, one is likely to study alongside others, or mothers of young children in a particular situation, one is likely to know more. If this works for your idea, just make sure that it does not mess up the mix you need by finding interviewees who are too similar.

Recruiting from an existing customer and/or user base

Up to now, we have been talking about a new idea for new customers and/or users. What about a new idea for an existing customer and/or user base? You have a gift! An existing customer base to recruit from! (You do need to be aware of any laws, regulations and best practice around data protection and consent when contacting your customer base.) Here are some ways that I have recruited from an existing customer base working with the client organisation.

Examples: How to recruit from an existing customer base

At a mobile operator, we first ran a report to identify customers who met the recruitment criteria. They displayed the required behaviours and characteristics based on their usage patterns and account information. Our sales teams then made outbound calls to recruit from the list during more quiet times. (Naturally, they had the necessary pre-agreements to contact them for research purposes.)

At the education company, the sales people routinely visited their customers, who were schools and colleges, so they were able to get a list of willing participants matching the criteria.

At a virtual world website, we added a box on the home page so that existing users could opt into our research. That was a good while ago, but these days it is very common practice to see the call out for potential interviewees on company websites and so on.

Keep one step removed from your interviewees

While I do encourage you to do your own recruitment if you can, please do stay at least one step removed. Ask your contacts to pass your call out message onto someone else and be clear that you are not asking them to take part in the research themselves. People you know directly are likely to carry bias. As my mother says, a skunk always smells beautiful to its mother! I have worked with clients who want you to recruit their friends and family members. While they are not direct contacts of yours, they are still probably too closely related to the initiator of the idea.

Create an effective call-to-action message

Whether you are using a screener, or just sending out a message for people to contact you for more information, you need to craft a clear call-to-action message that can easily be shared and sent around. You can think of it as an advert if you like. If you craft this message well, you will also be able to use it as an initial filter, which will cover one or two of your recruitment criteria. Below are some examples of simply crafted messages where you will see some demographic and situational elements in play and working as that first filter.

Example: Simple and effective call-to-action message for indoor market project

'Looking for a retail premise in <postcode>? Interested in a rent-free trial? <insert link to the screener questions>'

This message puts the call out using some of the situational criteria discussed earlier with the intention of cutting through to those who are genuinely interested. In this case, a screener is being used as there are a number of recruitment criteria and a particular mix of respondents is required.

Example: Simple and effective call-to-action message for taxi app project

Thinking about the example of a new taxi app, the hypothesis is all about improving the reliability of taxi services, so your call-to-action message could be:

'Think your taxi service could be better? Click here to take part in some paid research <insert link to the screener>'.

This message will attract only those people who have had bad taxi experiences so you know that you are starting with a potential interviewee who identifies with the problem. Again, in this example, I am suggesting that you push applicants through to a screener as there are likely to be quite a few recruitment criteria and additional demographic factors that will help you get the right mix. You will also note that in this case there is information that this is a paid research opportunity. This will make it clear that this is a call out for research rather than an advert by a taxi firm trying to lure people in! Naturally, also saying that this is paid research will be a big draw.

Example: Simple and effective call-to-action message for online study project

In this example you can see that this one message will work for recruiting both the customer and user group. The scenario is that you need to interview children (users) who were not able to study a subject that they want to at school and also their parents (the customer). In this situation, you can put the message out there addressed to the parents. This means that not only can you get them to help you with the recruitment of their child but also you can get their consent to interview the child if they are below a particular age. In this example, again, I would suggest a screener as there is going to be quite a few recruitment criteria plus information that you need to give around research best practice with minors.

'Has your child been unable to study a subject they wanted to at school? Click here to take part in some paid research <insert link to the screener>'

To pay or not to pay incentives

There is always a big debate over incentives. Having read the above examples, you are probably already questioning that yourself.

There are some circumstances where payment is not required. There are some circumstances where payment is not needed or appropriate. In my example of the indoor market project, potential test traders, I did not offer any incentive as there was a big potential future value for them. They would be eligible for a possible future rent-free test trade period.

Thank-yous rather than incentives. Sometimes, an incentive is not needed or appropriate, but it is nice to give the interviewee a thank you for their time. Not just because it is a respectful thing to do, but also what comes around goes around and at some future point you may want to re-engage with them. Of course, it does not always need to be cash. For example, I have sent food and wine hampers to the homes of senior managers who I video-interviewed, taken boxes of chocolates to company directors who I interviewed in their offices and bought cakes for the office to thank an estate agent for a thirty-minute chat. My Dad would offer a dozen golf balls, but that's another story!

Think carefully about paying interviewees for their time. For some reason, some innovators do not think that they need to pay interview interviewees. Some are concerned that paying them is in some way a bribe for getting them to say they like your idea. You are paying them for their time as they are doing a job for you, which is to have an open and honest conversation. By paying, you are showing that you value their input and respect their time. When you meet to carry out the research, you will explain that this honesty and openness is what you are paying them for. As you are paying them, they will want to do a good job for you and the honesty and openness will flow!

Slightly overpaying will get you a better show up rate! I also often hear from innovators that interviewees can be unreliable. I very rarely experience an interviewee not showing up for research as the payment is a good incentive. I would rather slightly overpay than scrimp on what I pay them as they are less likely to let you down if the incentive is good.

Travel considerations. If you are asking people to travel to your location you may need to think about paying a little more. Either way, it is best to communicate clearly that travel is included in the incentive. For some reason, many people have an idea that they will be reimbursed on top of the incentive. I have offered a lower incentive if I am travelling to interview people at their premises.

You may need to pay more for those with higher incomes versus students. You may also need to pay a little more for higher earners, such as professional people like accountants, business managers and HR people. At the other end of the spectrum, I have also carried out on-the-spot research with teens in coffee shops in North London and West Coast US and just picked up the tab for their coffee and cake.

Non-cash incentives. If you are carrying out research on behalf of a business, they may struggle to give you cash to pay your interviewees, so you could suggest online or physical vouchers as there will be a receipt which you can then put through expenses/accounts. If you are researching with an existing customer base who has a billing account with you or the client who commissioned the research, you could also consider that the incentive could be a credit on their account, or a discount on their next bill.

Example of recruitment criteria, call-to-action and screener

Here is an example from the indoor market project that shows a deliberately limited set of recruitment criteria that include both the demographic and situational elements, how the call-to-action message and a screener can work in practice.

Example: indoor market project, looking for potential test traders

Here is a reminder of the hypothesis: Our hypothesis is that we can generate full-price rentals in six months from all twenty empty shops, if the right mix of traders are given free test trading opportunities within a broader programme of activity.

Here is a reminder of the recruitment criteria for potential test traders:

- Eligible to trade in the UK (demographic)
- Old enough to sign up to a contract (demographic)
- Have a current product / service / experience suitable for a retail premise (situational)
- Are interested in a full-time retail opportunity to sell (or provide) their product or service (situational)

Gender, educational level and ethnicity are all examples of irrelevant recruitment criteria, although they may be important elements to make sure you get a good enough variety in the mix of interviewees.

With the call-to-action message, 'Looking for a retail premise in <enter postcode>? Interested in a rent-free trial? <insert link to the screener>', there is some initial filtering as you will be attracting people only interested in a full-time retail opportunity and if the location does not suit them, they will not apply. Be careful about making dangerous assumptions. If instead, you were to ask questions in your screener about where they lived and do your own filtering based on those who only live nearby, you could be limiting your audience unnecessarily. You can't assume that just because they don't live nearby, they are not interested. Perhaps they regularly stay with a partner or family member that lives nearby, perhaps they have no problem with travelling, many people do travel far to get to work, or perhaps they are renting and are flexible with where they live. Try not to be too limiting with your criteria or you could miss out a whole potential audience.

Getting the call-to-action message out there: This message will be shared on social media, with a special plea to like and re-share. It will also be sent to a list of relevant contacts majoring on those who run creator and community groups. Local press will also be approached to share the message. Message is also to be put out by council contacts in their monthly newsletter with a paragraph about the project.

The screener: As per my advice above, the reasons that a screener is being used here are as there are a few recruitment criteria with a number of variables for the mix plus there is some additional information to share.

Screener for potential test traders in the indoor market project	
Copy and questions for the screener	**Guidance**
We are the xx agency <insert webpage link>. We are working with the landlord of <insert name> indoor market <insert postcode>. They have some empty shop units and are considering giving away some rent-free test trade periods for people to try out new retail ideas in the hope that they will become permanent longer term tenants. To find out whether there is enough interest we are looking to have 1-hour in-person conversations with potential traders.	**Explain who you are and what this is all about.**

Screener for potential test traders in the indoor market project	
Copy and questions for the screener	Guidance
Below are a series of questions so we can see if you are a good fit for this project. If you are interested in this potential, then we will be in touch within the next five days as we would like to meet you and chat more about this.	**Tell them what you are going to ask them to do and what will happen next.**
Please be assured that we will not share your information with anyone outside of our project team at our agency.	**Give any information required by data protection regulations applicable in your country.**
Qu 1. The market hours are Monday to Saturday, 10 am to 5 pm. The landlords need to be sure that shop units are staffed at all times during the test trade period. If you were successful in your application, would you be able to ensure that those hours can be staffed? <Yes/No>	This is one of the **situational recruitment criteria** 'Are interested in a full-time retail opportunity to sell (or provide) their product or service'.
Qu 2. What is your age? <offer a drop-down list of age bands>	The question on age covers both one of the **demographic recruitment criteria** that they need to be able to enter into a legal contract by being over eighteen plus it gives you information to help you choose interviewees with a good range of ages to get your **mix** right.

Screener for potential test traders in the indoor market project	
Copy and questions for the screener	Guidance
Qu 3. Are you eligible to work in the UK? <Yes/No>	This is one of the **demographic recruitment criteria** 'Eligible to trade in the UK'.
Qu 4. What would you be selling in your shop? <short free text box>	This is one of the **situational recruitment criteria** 'Have a current product / service / experience suitable for a retail premise' and by using a free text box you will be able to make your own decision on the information you have been given about whether they fit or not. For example, selling cars does not work in the small space; there is a need to avoid anything that is too directly competitive with existing traders (e.g. fruit and veg) and it would be good to get a variety of offerings. This question is also important for the **mix.**
Qu 5. What is your gender? <insert drop down list>	This will help you choose a good **mix** of interviewees.

Screener for potential test traders in the indoor market project	
Copy and questions for the screener	Guidance
Qu 6. If you are interested in helping us find out if the free test trade opportunity is viable please fill out your contact details below so we can get in touch with you. Full Name Mobile Number Email Address	**Ask for their contact information** so you can get back to them.

Good practice when creating screeners

In the example above, you will see some things to cover in your screener. Here are some tips that may help you create a screener:

- Explain who you are and what this is all about to help applicants understand the context and to reassure them. Once they understand a bit more, they may decide that they do not fit. If you can, provide a link to any online presence that you have as it will help to reassure people.

- Explain why you are asking the questions and what you are going to do with the information they give you, along with any information required by data protection regulations applicable in your country.

- Include questions that get information for all your recruitment criteria (demographic and situational).

- Make sure that you get any additional information you need so you can select a good mix of interviewees.

- Ask for their contact information so you can get back to them: It is advisable to ask them to enter mobile number and email address twice as people can easily type them incorrectly.

Difficulties finding interviewees

If you are finding it difficult to find people who fit the recruitment criteria and mix, then you need to question how you are going to find them to sell to once your product is built.

(a) Is there something in your value proposition that is too narrow? This is likely to be either to do with the people who you are adding value for or to do with the problem, need or desire, so go back to Step 1 (Write hypothesis) and review your value proposition

or

(b) Are they just not within your reach and you need help? In which case you might consider going to an agency so you can go beyond your own networks

Using a recruitment agency

While I still recommend that you try and do the recruitment yourself, here is an outline of how recruitment agencies can work for you:

You may consider using an agency if you have access to funds (perhaps you work in a business), or if you find that it is difficult to access potential interviewees who fit your recruitment criteria and mix. An agency will commonly charge you a recruitment fee per head plus a project fee overall. The per head fee will be based on how easy or difficult the recruitment criteria are to fulfil. You can also expect to be charged a project fee. That will in itself tell you something about the potential size of your target customer and/or user groups. Most agencies can also handle the logistics too, organising the venue, sending out reminders and administering the interviewees' thank-you payments, all subject to extra costs of course.

You can choose a hybrid approach; for example, you could use an agency to find the interviewees and to make the arrangements of where and when to meet and you could handle the venue and interviewee payments yourself.

You give an agency both your recruitment criteria and desired mix. They will turn them into a screener that they use on phone conversations with potential interviewees, capturing all the answers as they chat. This serves a double purpose as they can also tell if the potential interviewee is chatty enough to be a good person to talk with. You too can always have a phone conversation with a potential interviewee before you confirm their involvement.

Completing The Really Good Idea Test templates

Are you working on your own idea as you go through this book?

If so, then you should still be using the CORE template.

You are now ready to complete Step 4 (Find interviewees), which is highlighted below.

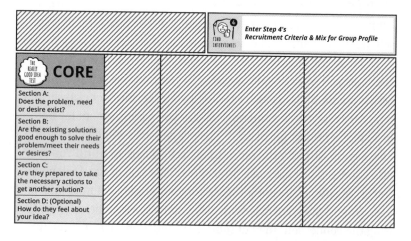

You will have completed Step 1 (Write hypothesis), Step 2 (Identify risks) and Step 3 (Create questions). You are yet to complete Step 5 (Measures and targets). You see all those sections are shaded.

What do I write in this box?

In this Step 4 (Find interviewees) box, you are going to enter your group profile. You can give the group profile a name, add the number you are going to interview, a summary of the recruitment criteria and the variables in your mix.

Here is an example of a completed Step 4 box for the potential test traders in the indoor market project.

Group Profile: 5 Potential Test Traders
-Eligible to trade in the UK
-Old enough to sign up to a contract
-Have a current offering suitable for a shop unit
-Interested in a full-time retail opportunity
-Mix: Age, gender, retail offering

FIND INTERVIEWEES

Remember that if you have different group profiles, for example, you have one customer group profile and one user group profile, that you need to create a different CORE template for each one.

Try it for yourself!

Remember you can download the templates from productdoctor.co.uk.

TOP TIPS

Start with just five interviewees

Go one step further and add a sixth wildcard who does not fit the group profile

Recruit interviewees yourself as you will learn a lot more about them

COMMON PITFALLS

Jumping straight to a survey and missing the value of face-to-face interviews

Limiting your customer and/or user profile by having too many recruitment criteria

Not having enough diversity in the group mix

STEP ⑤

MEASURES & TARGETS

KEY POINTS

Decide how you are going to measure the answers to the interview questions you ask

Set targets for an overall group so you know what scores constitute positive or negative evidence

In Step 2 (Identify risks) you work through your Step 1 (Write hypothesis) to discover where your assumptions are. You then grade some of the assumptions 'risky' as they are fundamental to the success of your overall idea and you feel that you do not have enough evidence to feel comfortable with the level of risk. In Step 3 (Create questions) you craft interview questions designed to get you evidence in the hope that you can reduce the risk level of those assumptions and feel more confident to move forward with your idea.

In Step 4 (Find interviewees) you develop some criteria to profile the customers and/or users who you think stand to benefit the most from your idea. You also work through how best to find and recruit them as you are getting ready to ask them your questions.

In this Step 5 (Measures and targets), measures are set that will help to assess and analyse the answers from each interviewee. Then group targets are set so that we know what scores across that group of interviewees constitute positive evidence. Positive evidence means that you can reduce the levels of risk in your assumptions, which will give you more confidence to make a decision whether to pursue your idea or not.

By the end of Step 5 you will be ready to move into the final stages of preparing for carrying out the research in Step 6 (Conduct interviews). If you have more than one group to interview, then each group profile will have its own set of risky assumptions, interview questions, recruitment criteria and measures and targets. If you are using the templates, you will create one CORE template for each different group.

The purpose of this step is to avoid a common pitfall of reviewing interviewees' answers with rose-tinted glasses on. Innovators often make a decision based on gut feel of how the interview went overall. If it is a good, flowing and lively conversation it can feel like a positive response overall, when in the cold light of day, it might not have been. It is also quite natural to try and hear the answer that you want to hear and it can be difficult to stay neutral. Putting in a scoring mechanism will help to reduce your own bias and help you stay as neutral as you can.

Despite this being a relatively small exercise, it is important enough to have its very own step!

Set individual measures

These measures are for each interviewee and set against each risky assumption that you have identified in Step 2 (Identify risks). The questions you have written are designed to get you information so that you can score each measure. The measures are there in an attempt to create an unbiased scoring mechanism.

It is advisable to keep these measures as simple as possible. They should be simple enough that you can assign a score in the interview itself.

Measures for section A: Does the problem, need or desire exist?

You could use a YES/NO measure here: YES the problem, need or desire exists or NO the problem, need or desire does not exist. However, this does not really help you with the level of pain and one of the key points behind whether the problem, need or desire exists is how strong it is. It may be better to choose a metric for section A answers that show the level expressed in a scale of 0–5, where 0 is no problem, need or desire exists and 5 is a big problem, need or desire exists.

Here is an example using the indoor market project with the group profile of the potential test traders. It shows how the 0–5 scale works as a measure in interview section A.

Example: Section A measures for the indoor market project, potential test trader interviews

The risky assumption in this example is that the profiled potential test trader group actually truly desires a longer term retail space to sell their offering. The questions being asked have been designed to get them to talk about where they have sold in the past and from their answers it will be possible to tease out how strong the desire is.

So the measure here is about whether the desire exists and to what level. It will be measured on a scale of 0–5, where 0 is no desire and 5 is a big desire.

Measures for section B: Are the existing solutions good enough to solve their problem/meet their needs or desires?

This measure can be kept simple with a YES or NO. The essence behind the question is whether the interviewee feels that there is room for another solution, or whether they feel that the existing offerings give them everything they need. The answers here also help to score the level of pain in section A.

Now in some cases, people don't know what they want until you show them an alternative. If you are showing them your idea for a solution in interview section D, you can use their answer in both interview section B and interview D to score the measure to this question.

Here is an example using the indoor market project with the group profile of the potential test traders. It shows how the scale works as a measure in interview section B.

Example: Section B measures for the indoor market project, potential test trader interviews

The risky assumption here in section B is whether there is room for another sales opportunity as it may be that the existing sales opportunities meet their needs. The questions in this case are designed to get the interviewee to talk about what is attractive or not about existing sales opportunities and to get them to describe their ideal opportunity. Through those answers, it will be possible to assess whether the shop unit offering in the indoor market can meet their desires better than what is already on offer.

One of the ways to measure the responses here is 'YES or NO' to whether the existing ways to sell meet their needs and desires. Now, you may think that they have already answered that question simply by having applied to take part in the research but this is an opportunity to learn more. All is never as it seems until you delve further! Remember that there is also more to learn here than just establishing the score for the

---

measure. You will hear all about the competition – in this case, other opportunities for potential traders, that would take their attention away from this project.

Measures for section C: Are they prepared to take the necessary actions to get another solution?

In this section you are looking for evidence that they will take the action(s) you require. The strongest evidence you can get will be that they have taken this action before. Remember that you can push for parallel situations, so it is that they have taken the action, albeit not in the exact context or way that you are thinking of. For example, the action is that you want a parent to spend money on a new app to distract their child while the parent gets on with their chores. So the action you are looking for in a broad sense is the spending of money to solve that problem. It does not need to be money spent on an app, it could be on a new toy or a babysitter.

This can also be a YES or NO measure. They have either taken the action(s) before or not. If you have more than one action here, then remember to add a measure for each one.

Here is an example using the indoor market project with the group profile of the potential test traders. It shows how the YES/NO measure works in interview section C.

Example: Section C measures for the indoor market project, potential test trader interviews

In this case the risks are around whether the interviewee is prepared to invest time and a little money (not for rent, but for the reduced rates and kitting out their shop unit) and whether they are able to work within an environment that is going to be continually changing. Test traders will come and go and there will be continual experimentation of new marketing ideas, events to attract visitors, pop-up activities and so on. Some will succeed and some will fail. The place will be in flux until all the empty shop units are on permanent leases. This is not like taking a shop unit on an established high street.

The first two questions ask potential test traders to give previous examples of where they have spent time and money previously, and of having operated in this sort of environment. There are additional questions that also ask how they feel about taking these actions in this context. They already know what the context is as they have applied to be interviewed about this and have seen more information about the project in the screener. So this means that while they may not be able to give you solid examples of having taken those actions before, they are likely to have a view on whether they are prepared to take them in this case.

There are two different measures to set here as there are two risks. These measures can simply be YES or NO, interviewee is/is not prepared to invest time and a little money and YES or NO, interviewee is/is not prepared to work in that environment.

Measures for section D: (Optional) How do they feel about your idea?

In this interview section, you will be sharing your new concept in order to get some feedback. It could be just a paragraph that describes it, or something a little more elaborate. The main risks here are that they do not like the solution that is being proposed.

The main questions are most likely going to be based around The Trilogy to tease out if there is anything in particular that appeals, anything that they have questions or concerns about, anything that they hope it will do or any improvements that they would make. As with all these measures, they need to be right for your particular hypothesis and circumstances so you may have other questions that address other particulars.

With The Trilogy questions in play, the feedback will go beyond being able to score this measure and will get into all the ways that the idea could be improved upon. However, for the purposes of this step and writing this initial individual measure, you may decide to use a scale or a YES/NO answer. It depends on the detail of the idea, solution or concept that you have.

Here is an example using the indoor market project with the group profile of the potential test traders. It shows how the measures can work in interview section D.

Example: Section D measures for the indoor market project, potential test trader interviews

In this case the risks are whether any of the empty shop units actually appeal to them and whether the terms, conditions and costs are acceptable. At this point in the interview, the interviewee will be taken into the market and shown the empty available shops and the paperwork and asked appropriately tailored versions of the Trilogy question.

The measures for the questions are firstly, a scale of 0–5 as a way to measure their interest in one (or more) of the empty shop units and a YES/NO/MAYBE measure on response to the paperwork. The MAYBE option allows for questions to be asked or suggestions made of changes to the paperwork.

In the example above, there is a YES/NO/MAYBE measure. It may feel right to add in a MAYBE answer and to think through what you would do with that response. During these interviews you are going to get lots of information beyond these scores that will help you to improve upon your proposition, tighten up your target groups and so on. You might see that the MAYBEs would be a YES, if you could implement changes that the interviewee suggested. So, if they are feasible, you could turn some of the MAYBEs into a YES or conversely, into a NO if they are not feasible.

Assigning a score for the measure

There are two opportunities to actually assign the individual score. The first is going to be during the interview itself, in Step 6 (Conduct interview), while it is fresh in your mind. The second is in Step 7 (Analyse and decide) when you go back over each interview and analyse what you have learned. I strongly recommend audio recording each interview and will discuss more in the next step.

With these measures, you can use the closing section of the interview conversation to check that you have enough information to assign a score and to check directly with the interviewee whether you have assigned appropriate scores. There is more about how to do that in Step 6 (Conduct interview).

Set group targets

Now you need to set a target score for each measure across the group. Once you have completed all the interviews in a group, you will be able to do a tally and see whether they hit their group target as a group, or not. Setting this target is a judgement call that must be based on your particular idea and market.

Example: Using judgement when setting group targets for indoor market project, potential test trader interviews

In the case of the potential test traders in the indoor market project, with five interviewees in the group, the group targets are out of five. Scores of three and four out of five for these measures feel like a strong enough result. With twenty shops in total to offer up for test trading and, say, a year of rolling test trades offered up to reach full occupancy, it feels about right. If only one was positive, then perhaps this would feel a bit too low.

There is always the opportunity to go to another five potential test traders, making any improvements or tweaks that you heard about in the first round, and see how a further group scores. If the first group of five interviewees were all scored positively, then in this case, I would be unlikely to take the test to a further group.

In this example, once again, using the indoor market project, the group targets are shown against the individual measures that were discussed above.

Example: Step 5 Measures and targets for the indoor market project, potential test trader interviews

Interview section	Step 2's risky assumptions	Step 5's individual measure	Step 5's group target
A	That they want a longer term retail space to sell their offering	0–5 desire for a long-term space	4/5 are 4+
B	That the existing ways to sell could be improved upon	YES or NO to a new way to sell	3/5 YES
C	1) Prepared to invest time and money into a new sales opportunity 2) Prepared for continual changing environment, trial and error	1) YES or NO prepared 2) YES or NO prepared	1) 3/5 YES 2) 3/5 YES
D	1) Shop units are appealing 2) Terms, conditions and costs are acceptable	1) 0–5 interest in a shop unit 2) YES, NO or MAYBE with feasible changes	1) 3/5 are 3+ 2) 3/5 YES or MAYBE

If the size of your potential audience is quite small – for example, if it is students who cannot study the subject that they want at school – then you may want a higher group target. If, on the other hand, you are looking at developing a new taxi service, then that is more of a mass market offering, so you may decide that only one out of five interviewees needs to be positive.

If you decide to add in a wildcard, then you will need to decide what to do with it regarding counting towards these scores. If your wildcard is a good fit for your idea and has shown you that your target group is different to what you thought it was, then by all means count them. If not, then leave them out of the scoring.

Avoid getting stuck! My overall advice here is to be bold. You need to just need to work out how you are going to measure the evidence you need and then what score makes it positive. Try not to overthink. Be realistic and really honest with yourself. Imagine that you are outside looking in. What sounds like a good measure to you that offers up some proof before you invest your money further developing your idea? What number makes it sound like it is a good idea to progress? I have seen people spend hours debating this. Don't overthink it. Just call it and move on as, guess what, you can go back and iterate as you go!

It is very likely, as with every step, that when you try to work out these targets, you will find yourself wanting to make changes to earlier steps. Perhaps this will be to your risky assumptions in Step 2 (Identify risks), or the questions that you are to ask in Step 3 (Create questions) or the group profiles in Step 4 (Find interviewees), or even to the way that you have framed your overall idea in the hypothesis (Write hypothesis). So by all means, please do go back through previous steps and make changes. Just remember that at whatever step you make the changes, you need to work back through the steps chronologically to get back here.

Completing The Really Good Idea Test templates

Are you working on your own idea as you go through this book?

If so, then you should still be using the CORE template.

You are now ready to complete the box for Step 5 (Measures and targets).

You will have completed Step 1 (Write hypothesis), Step 2 (Identify risks) and Step 3 (Create questions) and Step 4 (group profile). You can see all of those are shaded.

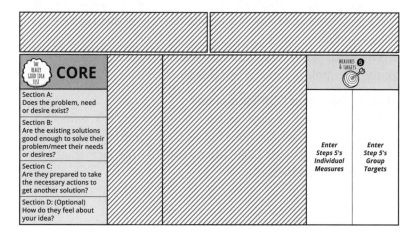

Once you have completed the boxes for Step 5 (Measures and targets), then you have a document that you may like to share with colleagues and stakeholders to explain your next steps. It is a summary and rationale of who you are going to interview, what you are going to ask them, why and how you are going to analyse their responses to see if you have passed The Really Good Idea Test.

This CORE document is also going to become part of your full research script when you carry out your interviews in Step 6.

What do I write in these boxes?

Individual measures This box is for the individual measures for each of the risky assumptions that you entered from Step 2 (Identify risks). Remember that these measures are set against the risky assumptions and that the interview questions are there to get you enough information from the interviewees to be able to give them each a score.

When you get to Step 6, you will be able to add in the individual scores for each interviewee.

Group targets This box is for the total score of the group that are in this group profile. Remember that these are the levels you need to reach to constitute whether your evidence is enough to reduce the risky assumption or not.

When you get to Step 7 you will be able to total up the scores across the whole group and add them in.

Time to share your CORE template?

The CORE template now has something in every box, reflecting all the work that has been done in Steps 1 through to 5. Here is an example of a completed CORE template for the indoor market project, potential test traders.

1 WRITE HYPOTHESIS

Our hypothesis is that we can generate full-price rentals in 6 months from all 20 empty shops if the right mix of traders are given free test test trading opportunities within a broader programme of activity

4 FIND INTERVIEWEES

Group Profile: 5 Potential Test Traders
- Eligible to trade in the UK
- Old enough to sign up to a contract
- Have a current offering suitable for a shop unit
- Interested in a full-time retail opportunity
- Mix: Age, gender, retail offering

3 CREATE QUESTIONS

5 MEASURES & TARGETS

THE REALLY GOOD IDEA TEST — CORE	2 IDENTIFY RISKS	3 CREATE QUESTIONS	5 MEASURES & TARGETS
Section A: Does the problem, need or desire exist?	That they want a longer term retail space to sell their offering	Where have you sold your <offering> in the past? Have you rented or considered renting retail premises? Are there any other sales opportunities that you have considered or are considering? What interests you about this particular opportunity?	0-5 desire for a long-term space — Target: 4/5 are 4+
Section B: Are the existing solutions good enough to solve their problem/meet their needs or desires?	That the existing ways to sell could be improved upon	Thinking about where you can sell today (a) What appeals about each opportunity? (b) Is there anything that concerns you? (c) Describe your ideal trading opportunity...	YES or NO to a new way to sell — Target: 3/5 YES
Section C: Are they prepared to take the necessary actions to get another solution?	1) Prepared to invest time & money into a new sales opportunity 2) Prepared for continual changing environment, trial & error	1) Can you give me any examples of where you invested time and money to make some sales? Do you have an example of when you were one of the first to try out a new sales opportunity? 2) Given what you know about this potential opportunity, are you prepared to invest time and a little money to get yourself set up as a trader? How do you feel about working within this new project where there is going to be a period of trial and error for everyone?	1) YES or NO prepared — Target: 1) 3/5 YES; 2) YES or NO prepared — Target: 2) 3/5 YES
Section D: (Optional) How do they feel about your idea?	1) Shop units are appealing 2) Terms, conditions & costs are acceptable	1) Let's go into the market and look at the empty shop units. (a) Are there particular shop unit(s) that appeal to you? (b) Do you have any questions? (c) Do you have any suggestions? 2) Take a look at this draft paperwork (a) Is there anything that you are pleased to see? (b) Do you have any concerns or questions? (c) Are there any changes you would propose?	1) 0-5 interest in a shop unit — Target: 1) 3/5 are 3+; 2) YES, NO or MAYBE with feasible changes — Target: 2) 3/5 YES or MAYBE

Try it for yourself!

Remember that you can download these templates from productdoctor.co.uk.

TOP TIPS

Set up measures and targets before conducting interviews as this will help you to be objective when analysing the interviewees' answers

Keep measures simple using YES, NO, MAYBE and/or simple 0–5 scales

Now you have filled out something in every box, you can use the CORE template document to communicate your journey and rationale before starting the interviews

COMMON PITFALLS

It is highly likely in carrying out this step, that you will want to make changes to previous steps. Go make them and get the most out of the test!

The measures need to be set against each risk, not each individual interview question. The interview questions are there to get you the information to assign a score for each measure.

Spending too much time over-thinking measures and targets. Just call it and move on!

STEP 6

CONDUCT INTERVIEWS

KEY POINTS

Get ready for the interviews, planning and checking all the logistics

Finalise your research script by adding an introduction, closing section and timings

See guidance on good practice to get the most out of the interview

In this step it is all about having the research conversations. The riskiest assumptions lurking in your hypothesis have been identified from Step 1 (Write hypothesis) and Step 2 (Identify risks). Questions to tease information from interviewees have been written in Step 3 (Create questions) and the interviewees have been profiled in Step 4 (Find respondents). Measures to score the evidence against the riskiest assumptions have been set up in Step 5 (Measures and targets). So now, in this Step 6 (Conduct interviews), you work through the logistics and finalise your group of interviewees, complete your full research script, review good practice and you are ready – go interview!

The key to good research interviews lies in making the interviewees feel comfortable so that they are open and chatty with you. This starts with the various assurances and explanations you have given them during the recruitment process. It carries on as you make arrangements to meet, through the language you use and the venue you choose and it all comes together (with any luck!) in the actual interview with various techniques to get them talking openly.

Logistics

Selecting the venue for the research interview

Can you meet in their natural environment? It is a great idea to carry out the conversation in the natural environment that your interviewees might be when they experience your offering. For example, if your idea is based around addressing a pain, need or desire that comes up when they are walking in the park, then go meet them on their walk. How about something that they will use when they are driving? You could go sit in the car with them. How about something that addresses a problem for them while they are working? You could go to their work desk. If it is something that they are going to do whilst sitting at their desk and being online, then you may find that a video call is ideal as you can see their surroundings.

When you interview people in their natural environment, you will get extra details about their lives that you may not get if you put them in another environment. You might actually be able to see the problem and also see what solutions the interviewee has tried to put in place. It will be easier for the interviewee to talk them through if they can show you. Think for example, about how difficult it is to design a garden if you are not standing in it. Of course, I am not encouraging you, or taking any responsibility for you putting yourself in any unsafe situations with people you have not met before, but you see the point!

Meeting over video

I am sure you will already know and use a number of services offering video calling. The most important consideration is to select one that your interviewee is comfortable with. So, when you make the arrangement to meet, you can ask them which they are happy to use. You can of course also add this question to your screener. You may like to steer them to your preferred one. For example, while there are other ways to record the conversation and share documents, I do like to use those that have that functionality built in.

Free venues

If you are going to meet face-to-face, in person, you may like to consider these free venues.

A meeting room in your office is fine as long as you are not trying to be anonymous and your reception and security will let them into the building. I have also used friend's offices and the interviewees' office. If you are visiting someone in their office, ask them to book a meeting room so you get peace and quiet.

I have used hotel lounges and coffee shops. While you might try to avoid particularly busy times of the day like lunchtimes, you will never know whether they will be suitable until you arrive, or worse, when you start the session. If I am using one of these, I always go and check them out beforehand and have a conversation with whoever is in charge. I let them know what I am doing and also check whether there is anything particularly noisy planned that I should avoid. Naturally, I also make it clear that I will buy a drink and a snack for myself and each interviewee. I have had incidents where I had to move when a large group turned up half-way through a research session, but that is the trade off in using public spaces.

My kitchen table has served me quite well over the years for research groups. Comfortable, quiet and easy to park. Again, from a safety point of view, I take no responsibility for you doing that. You can of course organise for someone else to also be at home when you do the interviews!

Small-budget venues. If you have some budget, you may like to hire a space as you will avoid some of the unknown perils of public places. This is also good if you are trying to keep anonymous. There are many spaces that will offer hourly or half-day to a day increments. You are more likely to find these advertised in cities and busy towns rather than more remote spaces. However, even if they don't advertise their space, pubs and other places with private rooms are often happy to come to an arrangement. I have hired private rooms in pubs, restaurants (outside of meal times), office meeting rooms and hotel meeting rooms to conduct interviews.

Big-budget venues. You can use a full-on research facility. You will be able to find them quite easily if you search online. Research facilities will cost more, but they will have reception staff who will meet and greet your interviewees, handle the payments and any pre-research signatures you may need. They will organise refreshments and also offer you videotaping and facilities for more technical usability techniques, such as eye tracking if you need them. For a one-to-one interview, a research facility does feel a bit like overkill, so a small quiet meeting place is often the best option.

Is a colleague or client insisting on joining the interview?

The rule of thumb is that you do not overpower the interviewees in numbers as it can be intimidating for them and you want the conversation to be as open and natural as possible. Here are some options: you could ask your colleague or client if they are happy to listen to the audio after the event. If that is not enough, then okay, perhaps they are happy to watch a video? You can of course set up a video recording yourself (obviously, this would need to be in one of the more private environments) using your mobile phone positioned accordingly, or you could use a bigger budget research venue. If that is not good enough, then the research venues will have rooms with a two-way mirror. That means that they can watch without the interviewees seeing them sitting behind that mirror. You do, however, need to tell the interviewees that they are being watched, which again, can be intimidating for some people. It's not all bad though, there is also an obvious benefit of having a colleague or client with you – they could suggest questions around things you had not picked up on during the interview yourself. If you do have an observer, ask politely that they keep all questions until the end of the interview and let the interviewees know that is happening.

Tips for selecting a venue for a physical face-to-face interview

- Check the venue is easy enough to get to.

- If you are not near public transport, ensure you and your interviewees have somewhere to park and/or be dropped off.

- Make sure that there is a comfortable space for a conversation with a table on which to put your audio recorder and for you to easily refer to your research script.

- Check internet access and mobile signal before you go if you require them for the interview. Have a back up to your plan and have printouts, or videos that have been saved to your hard drive rather than relying on internet access.

- Ensure any electronic equipment is fully charged, checking also that you have access to plug sockets at the venue if required and remember to take your chargers with you!

- Snacks can be a good idea and at the very minimum, provide a (soft) drink as you are hopefully going to be getting the interviewees to talk a lot! Best to avoid chewy toffees or other mouth-filling, crunch-making food!

- Try to avoid noisy and busy venues where it is not only difficult to hear what is being said, but which also cause problems when you try to listen back to your audio.

Arranging to meet interviewees

You will need to have a dialogue with the interviewees to make arrangements to meet. In my opinion, it can be beneficial to be able to have that conversation over the phone as it is quicker than writing to each other, going back and forth, but also as there seems to be more commitment when you actually speak. I suggest that you also confirm the details in writing and then send another reminder up to twenty-four hours before you are due to meet, asking them for a final confirmation. If you are concerned about someone not showing, you can also send a reminder that same day and ask them to message you back to confirm. It is probably best to use email for confirmation if it includes more lengthy information such as venue directions or any instructions about pre-work, as you have more room to write.

Here is a summary of things to include in the communication to those who you want to interview. They include both practical and best-practice research and data privacy regulations and guidelines. Do please check your local regulations and guidelines.

- Thank them for offering to be interviewed.

- Mention any preparation that they need to do and anything they need to bring to the research with them.

- Confirm the incentive.

- If you are physically meeting, then tell them when and where to meet. Make sure you give the interviewees very clear instructions so that they know where to find you and what will happen when you meet. If for example, you are meeting them in an office reception, then let them know whether they need to go and tell the receptionist that they are here, or whether they just sit down and wait for you. This is all about making the interviewees feel comfortable.

- If you are physically meeting, then suggest they arrive early and outline what they can expect when they arrive.

- Tell them how long the research session will be.

- Tell them the purpose of the research is and what you will do with the results (explain and honour confidentiality).

- Ask for any permissions required by regulation, for example, to audio record or take photographs or use anonymous quotes in documents for marketing purposes. (You can find samples of consent forms online if you wish to use them) If you are showing anything particularly confidential, and want them to sign a non-disclosure agreement, then send it to them beforehand. (I very rarely need to do this.)

- Give your mobile number and ask for theirs. It is important that you both have each other's mobile numbers if there are any issues on the day.

Here is a sample email confirmation for the indoor market project example, potential test traders interviews. This assumes you have had a conversation to agree on the time and place.

Example: Email confirmation for indoor market project interviewees

(Title) Research on <insert date> about retail space in the indoor market

I'm really pleased that you are able to meet me for the research conversation about shop units in the indoor market.

Please can you bring with you any samples or photos of your <insert reference to the idea for the shop unit, product or service that they told you about in the recruitment screener>.

We have agreed to meet on Wednesday 15th May at 4pm. We will be finished by 5pm. Location: 'XY Coffee' which is opposite XY Station on Station Road NW1 XYX.

I will put a red scarf on my table so will you know it is me.

By all means, feel free to arrive early, as we do want to start at 4 pm sharp. You may see me finishing up my previous research conversation, so please do grab a drink and hang on! I will definitely be ready for you at 4pm.

As you know, I will be making an audio recording of the conversation which is just for my benefit when I am writing up the conversations. I will not be sharing it with anyone outside of the project team. I will be writing up all the feedback from these conversations to share with the broader project team. Please be assured that I will not share any of your personal information.

If for any reason you cannot now make this time, please let me know so I can make alternative arrangements.

> *My mobile number is xxxxx. Please can you send me yours just in case we have any issues on the day?*
>
> *Look forward to meeting you*
>
> *Best*
> *Julia*

In this case, the interviewees are not being paid for their time as the benefit of a potential test trade period is quite high. If you are paying them, be sure to confirm that, for example. 'I will be giving you £x as a thank you for your time.'

Please do get back to everyone, including those people who do not meet your criteria. Not only is it good practice, but they may be your users or customers (in this case, market punters or temporary projects at a later date). Your response to the unsuccessful applicants could be something like:

> *Thanks so much for applying to join our research. We've had a lot of applications so I'm afraid we can't include you on this occasion. Hope to catch you next time.*
>
> *<insert name / company if you gave it>*

When I am carrying out one research session after another, I usually allow ten minutes leeway for people to arrive late plus another ten minutes break for me to go grab a cup of tea. So remember to add in some extra comfort time!

Starting the interview: The introduction

Here is an example script based on the indoor market project, potential test traders. It is based on a checklist which you may like to use to help you craft all research interview introductions. You may find it easier to write out your full script beforehand rather than freestyle it there and then.

Example: Script for the introduction section of the potential test traders interviews for the indoor market project

Thanks for agreeing to be part of this research.

I just want to firstly check that you can legally trade in the UK and that you are over 18?

We are going to spend around an hour talking about this idea of a rent-free test trade period in the indoor market.

As a researcher, I am not looking for any particular answers from you, there is no right and wrong. I have done my job well if I can get really honest feedback from you.

You will be able to see the timer on my audio recorder. Is it ok if I switch that on now? It is so that I can concentrate on the conversation we are having and listen back later. I will not share it with anyone else.

So your idea for a shop unit is <insert>. Have you managed to bring it along with you or a photo of it so you can talk to me a bit more about it?

Here is a checklist that you can use for the research interview introduction:

- Scribble down the timings for each section of the interview
- Check that they meet your recruitment criteria
- Give the incentive and explain what you need from them
- Set out your neutrality
- Explain what will happen
- Turn audio recorder on
- Use conversation opener to get the interviewee talking

Let's delve a little further into each point:

Scribble down the timings for each section of the interview

Your whole research script consists of an introduction, three or four sections and a closing. Work out how you are going to apportion the interview time between each section. Before you start each interview write down the start and end time for each section. This will help you pace the interview and avoid running out of time, which is very easy to do! Remember to add in the time for the interview introduction, which includes getting settled, and the closing.

Before I start the interview, I actually write down the timings according to when I start the interview, so if I start at ten in the morning I would scribble down 10–10.05 for the introduction, 10.05–10.15 on section A, 10.15–10.30 on section B and so on. Then I don't have to work out when I started and where I am while I am actually carrying out the research. You will find that certain interview sections take longer or shorter than you expected, so as you do more interviews, you can change your timings. As everything in this process, it is iterative and you can change and adapt as you move forward.

Check that they meet your recruitment criteria

Remember in your recruitment criteria that you had both demographic and situational elements? Well before you hand over any incentive, you are best to check that they do fit your recruitment criteria. If they don't, you have the option to send them away as you have not started the interview yet and (if relevant) have not paid the incentive yet. You may however still want to continue the interview as they may play the role of your 'wildcard' (see Step 4 Find interviewees).

Give the incentive and explain what you need from them

I like to give the incentive upfront so that the interviewees do not spend the interview time thinking about whether they will actually get paid. Some interviewees think that you will only pay them if you give them the responses that you want to hear and others will be worried about whether you remember to do it, so paying upfront removes those concerns. Then they can concentrate entirely on the conversation you are having. It is also good to pay them at the same time as you explain the importance of being open and honest as it will reinforce that this is the most important thing they can do, and essentially what you are paying them for.

I often hear the argument that incentives can bias a response, but the most important point I want to emphasise here is that you are paying them to be totally honest with you, not to tell you what they think you want to hear. Please do make that very clear in your introduction by looking deep into their eyes and saying that piece slowly!

Set out your neutrality

Make sure you look the interviewees right in the eye (again!) when you explain the importance of this point as this needs to register. Firstly, you are explaining what your role is in the broader context of the research and secondly, you are explaining the honesty that you need from them.

You will get the best out of interviewees if they think that you are totally impartial and not looking for any particular answer. If I am working on an idea I have created, then I often just say *I am researching this idea, so my job is to get the most open and honest feedback*. Then you are setting yourself apart from being the inventor. I also quite like saying this out loud to get myself into role. It helps me to get into character and act neutrally rather than veer into selling mode. It is method acting at its finest! Whatever you decide to say to set out your impartiality, you need to distance yourself from the product in front of the interviewees and also convince yourself that you are neutral.

When I worked for a mobile phone company, I never told hairdressers or taxi drivers where I worked as they would want to talk to me about problems and questions they had regarding their mobile phone service and I could not get away! If you are researching with existing customers and/or users, it is useful to be able to put this distance between you and the product, otherwise you may find yourself listening to customer gripes and unable to get to the information that you need.

Explain what will happen in the interview

They might have forgotten what was in the email or not read it properly. This is a good opportunity to outline what is going to happen. Some interviewees might be feeling a bit nervous. They can feel a bit like they are in a test environment and you are going to judge what they say.

To make them feel at ease, tell them that there are no right or wrong answers, remind them how long the session is going to take and invite them to check the timer at any time. It is worth also just explaining what you are going to do and how you have structured the interview. You can reference the start of a new section as you go through the interview to help orientate the conversation.

Turn audio recorder on

Have you tried to listen in a meeting and make notes at the same time? It is difficult to do, especially if you are trying to have a conversation and pick up on all the unspoken communication when your eyes are down. While you are busy writing notes you are missing that they have shifted uncomfortably in their chair and the conversation will also become more stilted and unnatural as you both have to wait for you to finish writing before moving on.

The audio recorder is your most important tool as a researcher. If you are interviewing over video, there may be recording functionality that you can use. Otherwise, you can use a separate recording device or the functionality on your phone. Make sure that you have tested it before the interview, that you have enough storage space and that you have spare batteries with you or full charge if you are using the recorder on your mobile phone.

Referencing the fact that you are going to record in the introduction will also serve as a reminder for you to press record. Yes, I have been there before and forgot to press the button!

Use a conversation opener to get the interviewee talking

You have an opportunity very early on in this conversation to get them talking on a subject that they know very well – themselves! You can also use this as a way to check their profile as some people can stretch the truth to get on to research. (This has only happened to me twice, ever.) You probably already know quite a bit about the interviewee, so it is the perfect way to start with a question like *When you applied to be part of this research you said that you . . . tell me a bit more about that?*.

This works both as a nice introduction to them and a way to get them comfortable talking with you. Most people love talking about themselves and it puts them at ease to see that you are so interested in what they have to say! So, all the more reason to start off by telling them that you have been paying attention to what they have already told you during recruitment. Your preparation shows respect and will also immediately set the tone for the nature of this conversation. You are showing that you are really interested in what they have to say.

This is also quite a good opportunity to ask a few more questions to help you build up a better picture of who they are. I would suggest that you leave any particularly personal questions (like age or marital status) to the end, once you are more familiar with each other.

Remember that you have limited time for the overall interview and you need to use it wisely

I have seen interviewers waste precious time on irrelevant things at this early stage. So there is little point wasting questions just because you want to make the interviewee feel comfortable. Each question you ask is being asked for a reason. You are only asking these questions because you need the answers and you need to make sure you have built in time to do this.

Good practice for research conversations

This section will help you to stay as neutral as you can in the interview as you want to avoid influencing the interviewees' answers.

Put on your 'research face'

I learned very early on the importance of 'research face'. Are you an enthusiastic character with an expressive face? Do you wear your heart on your sleeve? Your challenge is how to mask your emotions and appear totally dispassionate, without of course, appearing to be uninterested or unfriendly. It is time to get into character. Think about wearing a neutral expression. Your body language needs to follow, so be conscious if, for example, you cross your arms when you start to hear things you may not want to. Convince yourself that you have no investment in this idea at all. Don't blow your cover: You told them you were neutral, so be neutral!

Do not talk for more than 20 per cent of the time

You will get better at talking less, the more research conversations you have. When you listen back to your audio, you can take a measure of how much you have been talking versus how much you were listening. My rule is that you should only talk for 20 per cent of the time, maximum (that is excluding the introduction where, of course, you will be the main talker!) If you are talking more than that, then generally, you are probably trying to sell an idea or trying to encourage the interviewee to give you a particular answer.

Repeat back what they tell you

Active listening is a technique of repeating back something that a person says to you as a way to ensure that you are listening carefully to what they are saying. It will help you make sure you have heard what they actually said and not what you want to hear. It is a really useful thing to do in a research conversation as it also helps you to make sure that you have actually heard something correctly, especially if it is a crucial piece of information. It is also a great way to stay on a topic and dig further.

Here is how you can probe with active listening:

You said that the website you were using was really slow, so you left before you had a chance to make a payment. Is that right? (Pause for response) Apart from your frustration over the speed, was there anything you liked about the website?

Be sure to ask follow-up questions

When interviewed, interviewees are going to give you lots of information that is going to be relevant to your idea. Sometimes information that is going to be really important for you is only hinted at, or mentioned as an aside by an interviewee, so you need to make sure that you listen carefully enough to know when to probe further. I think of these nuggets as clues and your job is to spot them and remember to ask follow-up questions. You won't be able to pre-empt them in the interview questions that you draft, but being able to probe further when necessary will need to become a natural part of your research style. Not only will you need to listen closely to what an interviewee says, but also observe the emotion in how the interviewee is saying it and what their body language is telling you.

When you are doing this, try to prompt rather than tell the interviewee how they feel or leading them to an answer that you want to hear. Here are some questions you may use to probe further to access more information:

You said that X,Y,Z, can you tell me a bit more about that?

You seem to find that memory funny – why was that?

Your expression suggests to me that was not a good experience – did I read that right? (Pause for response) In what way was that not good?

You seemed to hesitate in giving that answer – why is that?

(if they are silent and appear to be thinking something through) Can you talk me through what you are thinking right now?

To avoid hypotheticals, find ways to get them to give you real examples

In Step 3 (Create questions) we talked about the dangers of asking hypothetical questions that prompt hypothetical answers. When carrying out the interview, we also need to avoid hypothetical discussions that are easy to fall into when you are in the natural flow of a conversation which will take you away from your original script. So you need to think about the technique of getting them to talk about real examples when you feel that hypotheticals are getting in the way.

Hypothetical answers will be given if you ask questions like: *How do you usually feel when that happens* or *What do you usually do in that situation*. Avoid these by asking questions like:

When did that last happen?

What did you feel when that happened

Can you give an example of that happening within the past 6 months.

Can you think of another example of that over the past year?

Earlier on, you talked about xxx, did you feel like this then too?

Remember that some of those examples may need to be fresh (depending on the context of your idea), so think about whether you ask them to give an example from the past few days or weeks rather than months or years.

Avoid second-hand information

In the main, you are better to steer interviewees to talk about themselves and their own experiences, rather than talking on behalf of someone else. You will find that interviewees say things like, *I am fine with it, but my friends hate it when that happens.* To which I would respond, *That's interesting but I need to keep this conversation about you* and move on. Getting second-hand information is not anywhere near as reliable as getting it first hand. One person cannot talk about how another feels with any great confidence.

Having said that, this interviewee may of course play an important role. Think back to the 'people map' in Step 1 (Write hypothesis). Maybe they are an important influencer, or introducer? Maybe they are the customer and not the user? To find this out, ask some further probing questions. For example, you may want to ask:

> *Can you tell me the last time that you recommended a <insert the category that we are talking about> to this person and they actually bought it / or started using it?*

Try to chat naturally, as you would with a friend

The best research interviews end up feeling as if you have just had a chat with a friend. The worst are stilted. I was once doing a series of interviews with parents and their children. A lady came to be interviewed on the first day and then returned on the second bringing her daughter with her for her interview, along with a bottle of wine for me. She was so thrilled that she had been paid to have such a good chat that she wanted to thank me. How lovely! Part of being natural is to get conversational, so avoid using jargon or difficult language. Just relax!

Remember also that you have invited them to the interview; you are the host, so it is up to you to set the tone. In general, I find that you get back what you push out, so the more open and chatty you are, the more likely you are to get that back. If you feel guarded, you will get that back too, so behave as you want them to behave with you.

Know when to back off

If you are getting answers that are beginning to show you that your idea is not as good as you hoped it was, then try not to fall into the trap of pushing them to give you the answer that you want! Instead, try and ask questions that will help you to work out why they do not fit your ideal target profile or that help you find a different context in which they have this problem or need. I would certainly persevere with the interview as you may find out something you did not expect.

This is another reason why I suggest that you start with just five interviews. So if you get negative responses from this initial group, you have not lost too much and you have also learned something really important, which is why your idea does not work for a particular group. I would still suggest completing all five interviews to confirm your suspicions. Your group target may be that three interviewees need to respond positively, so if the negative response happens on the first three interviews, you may be tempted to stop. Please don't! Negative responses are very important evidence to have as they help you work out whether you should make some changes and keep pursuing the idea, or stop working on it all together. Plus, you don't know what the last two interviewees will say to help you further shape your proposition.

Be prepared to shut down irrelevance to avoid wasting time

I know that it is rude to interrupt people when they are talking, but when you are paying them to talk to you, and you do it nicely, then it is not! They want to give you what you need, as you are paying them, so don't worry about doing it.

Here is a way to phrase it:

> *Sorry to interrupt, but this is outside the scope of this research, so instead can you tell me more about . . .*
>
> *I have heard you say that x, so let's move on now to y . . .*
>
> *Thanks for that. Now tell me about. . . .*

Don't answer their questions!

When you show interviewees something or describe an idea to them, some will ask you questions about it. While this is in itself a great indication that they have a problem, need or desire, please do resist from answering. If you start to answer you will be getting deeper into describing your idea and you will be missing the opportunity to find out from them what they want it to do. You could also find yourself wasting precious interview time. So if you get asked a question, and it is something that you want to know more about, then you can ask them what they want it to do and move on. So, for example, you could ask *What would you like the answer to be?*

If you are not interested in that particular element, then you can park the point and then get the interviewee to tell you other questions that they have. It is worth asking, as those questions may be stopping them from concentrating fully on answering your questions. So, for example, *That's an interesting question. What other questions do you have?*

Closing the interview

Here is a checklist that you can use for closing the interview:

- Check you have enough to assign scores for each target.
- Check your understanding of other important insights.
- Clarify any notes that you made during the interview.
- Get permission to recontact if appropriate.

Let's delve a little further into each point:

Check you have enough to assign scores for each target

Here is your chance to review the scores for the individual measures that you have set against each section of your interview. Can you decide on the score that you would assign there and then? Or do you need more information from the interviewee? Now is your chance to ask more questions before they leave! You can summarise what you have heard back to them and see if you have got it right.

You may want to even ask a very direct question to see what they think their score should be. For example, in the indoor market project for the potential test traders, this measure was a YES or NO answer:

You talked about all the sales opportunities that you have considered and from what you have said, I think that you are definitely interested in the right sort of longer term retail space. Did I understand you correctly?

If you have a question that has a scale as its measure, you could say something like:

We talked a lot about the problem of <enter context>. On a scale of 0–5, where 0 is no pain and 5 is very painful, how painful do you find it when that happens?

You can have a good summary discussion as you can refer back to information they have given you to see if you both think that the score is accurate.

Check your understanding of any other important insights

In addition to being able to put an individual score against the targets, there is going to be lots of other information coming from these interviews that is going to help you improve on your original value proposition statements. Remember the value proposition structure? This was the starting point in Step 1 (Write hypothesis) that has led you to this point:

For	Who has the need/problem/desire?
Who	What problem/need/desire do they have that you think you can solve?
Our	What generic product/service category does this fall into?
Gives	What benefit can you deliver them?
Unlike	How does it differ from/improve upon what is available today?

It works well to repeat back what you have heard and then check that you heard it correctly. Here is an example:

So to summarise, you have told me that you have a problem with x and that you would like something that does y – right?

I have found interviewees really good at correcting me here and putting this into their own words.

Clarify any notes that you made during the interview (using a pen and paper)

I am very strong on the point of audio recording the whole conversation so you don't need to take notes and can concentrate on what is being said. If you are doing video interviews, then you may find that there is a recording function. However, there will be times when you do need to make a note. You may want to remind yourself of something that has been said or you think of something else you want to ask. Stopping to delve further there and then might derail the conversation and ruin the flow. Make a note that you can come back to later. You may find it useful to time stamp or reference the interview section to help you remember what it relates to so that it is easy to refer back to at the interview closing and when you come to analysing the session in Step 7 (Analyse and decide). You may find it useful to scribble on to the relevant section of the research script itself.

Please do go 'old school' and use a pen and paper, not an electronic device. If you must use a phone or laptop in the session, for example to show material, then tell them what you are doing as your interviewees may think you are not listening and checking your messages instead which will disrupt the natural conversation!

It is also possible that you are talking to someone who likes to articulate something by drawing. I would not announce that there is a pen and paper for them to do that and I would also not put them within their reach, as this could be distracting, but you will notice that they will naturally reach for them if they want them.

Get permission to recontact if appropriate

If you find a good target user and/or customer match then get agreement to recontact them to help you in further research sessions. According to regulations in most countries, you would need to tell them what the research would be for, so you could say something like:

Can I recontact you for further research sessions about this particular idea?

By the end of the interview if your idea really appeals, they might ask you, unprompted, to let them know when it is available to buy or they may offer you further help. This has happened quite a few times in various projects and shows that you have really hit the mark! For example, when researching elements of this book, I had serious offers to proofread, which of course I accepted very gratefully (and I have added my thanks in the final chapter)!

Practice interviewing

It is definitely worth having a few practice runs now that you have your full research script. My suggestion is that you do this up to three times. You can do this with people you know and ask them to play the role of a particular target group.

As you practice the interviews with your research script you are most likely to find that you want to make changes to the questions. Perhaps you want to change the order, or the way that they are worded to make the conversation flow better. You will need to see how the interview works to time and you may need to trim the number of questions. I usually settle at a script that feels like a natural conversation after three practice interviews, so it is better to do this before you start for real. You will also get an idea of what research behaviours you need to work on. You can of course ask your practice interviewee to deliberately try to talk too much about what they did last night so you can practice getting the conversation back on track and so on.

Here is a format that you may like to use to get a good few practices in:

The Interviewer's Workout

Grab two people to help you practice. Ask one to be an interviewee and the other to be an observer. If you are struggling to find an observer, you could audio record the conversation and then go back and critique your own performance.

Brief the interviewee on who they are, giving them your recruitment criteria so they can get into character.

The observer must stay quiet. Their job is to watch you interview and then give you feedback on what you did well and what you could improve. Also ask the interviewee for feedback.

Here is a list of questions you can give the observer (you got it: 'The Trilogy'!)

(a) *Is there anything I did well on?*

(b) *Is there anything I did not do so well on?*

(c) *What could I improve?*

You can also give them this prompt sheet to help them critique you:

- How much did I talk vs the interviewee? (20 per cent is the most you are allowed to talk!)
- Did I ask follow-up questions to pick up on relevant things they said?
- Did I allow the conversation to get into hypotheticals where I could have asked them to use real examples?
- Were my questions constructed in a way that made them easy to answer?
- Did any of my questions feel leading – that I was looking for a particular answer?
- Did I focus on the solution (section D) before making sure I had fully explored the problem, existing solutions and potential actions (sections A, B and C)?
- Did the conversation overall feel natural?

You can also ask the interviewee how they felt being interviewed, using The Trilogy to tease out what you did well, not so well and where you could improve.

Reflect also on whether you managed to keep the conversation on track, steering the interviewee to give you information you want rather than letting them meander off the point.

Completing The Really Good Idea Test templates

Are you working on your own idea as you go through this book?

If so, then you can now use and complete the CHECKLISTS template. This one pager works with the CORE template and together they become the full research script that you can take into the research interview with you.

THE REALLY GOOD IDEA TEST — **6** CONDUCT INTERVIEWS — **CHECKLISTS**	Interviewee: Group Profile: Date/Venue: Interview Time: Interviewer:	*Enter info before the interview*	*Enter what you already know about the interviewee before the interview*
Introduction Checklist ☐ Scribble down timings on CORE ☐ Check recruitment criteria fit ☐ Ref. incentive & what you need	☐ Set out your neutrality ☐ Explain what will happen ☐ Turn audio recorder on ☐ Use conversation opener		**Closing Checklist** ☐ Have you scored each measure? ☐ Check important insights ☐ Permission to re-contact if applicable ☐ Clarify any notes you made
Introduction Script: *Add your script before the interview*			**Summary of Interviewee's Response:** *Write in here at the end of the interview*

What do I write in these boxes?

Before you go into the interview you can complete information that you already have about the interviewee. This will help to remind you when you are conducting the interview and do that important job of showing the interviewee that you have been paying attention to what they have already told you.

It is also important to make sure you add the interviewer's name (particularly important if there is more than one of you conducting them) and the other logistical information for good record keeping when you need to refer back at a later stage.

Here is an example of how the CHECKLISTS template would look after you have completed an interview. You will see information that needs to be completed before starting; including details about the interviewee and interviewer and the typed introduction script that corresponds to the checklist shown. You will also see the handwritten notes made at the end of the interview that summarise the interviewee's response.

CHECKLISTS

THE REALLY GOOD IDEA TEST

6 CONDUCT 2. INTERVIEWS

Interviewee:	Joanna Smith
Group Profile:	Test Traders 1
Date/Venue:	08/08
Interview Time:	1 hour
Interviewer:	Julia Shalet

Introduction Checklist

☐ Scribble down timings on CORE
☐ Check recruitment criteria fit
☐ Ref. incentive & what you need

☐ Set out your neutrality
☐ Explain what will happen
☐ Turn audio recorder on
☐ Use conversation opener

Closing Checklist

☐ Have you scored each measure?
☐ Permission to re-contact if applicable

☐ Check important insights
☐ Clarify any notes you made

Introduction Script:

Thanks for agreeing to be part of this research. I just want to firstly check that you can legally trade in the UK and that you are over 18?

We are going to spend around an hour talking about this idea of a rent-free test trade period in the indoor market. As a researcher, I am not looking for any particular answers from you, there is no right and wrong. I have done my job well if I can get really honest feedback from you.

You will be able to see the timer on my audio recorder. Is it ok if I switch that on now? It is so that I can concentrate on the conversation we are having & listen back later. I will not share it with anyone else.

So your idea for a shop unit is specialist hampers & locally sourced/made deli products. Have you managed to bring it along with you or a photo of it so you can talk to me a bit more about it?

Offering specialist hampers + homemade + locally sourced deli.

Previously sold in local fetes and catering for local events.

Have been looking for a retail opportunity but not found anything suitable.

Summary of Interviewee's Response:

Partnership between an experienced chef + experienced public sector innovator.

Eligible + very interested.

Idea seems unique so far.

Have been looking for a retail space.

Well networked online with a good social media. Good local marketing connections.

Just before you start, and based on the time that you begin, you can handwrite the timings on the CORE template against each section, not forgetting to add in also your introduction and closing section timings.

During the interviews, you can also add the individual scores against the measures (see the first column under Step 5 Measures & targets). You do not need to do anything with the final column at this stage.

Here is an annotated CORE template where you can see both the handwritten timings and the scores against the measures from one interview.

1 — WRITE HYPOTHESIS

Our hypothesis is that we can generate full-price rentals in 6 months from all 20 empty shops if the right mix of traders are given free test trading opportunities within a broader programme of activity

4 — FIND INTERVIEWEES

Group Profile: 5 Potential Test Traders
- Eligible to trade in the UK
- Old enough to sign up to a contract
- Have a current offering suitable for a shop unit
- Interested in a full-time retail opportunity
- Mix: Age, gender, retail offering

THE REALLY GOOD IDEA TEST / CORE	2 — IDENTIFY RISKS	3 — CREATE QUESTIONS	5 — MEASURES & TARGETS	
Section A: 10–10.05 Intro 10.05–10.15 Does the problem, need or desire exist?	That they want a longer term retail space to sell their offering	Where have you sold your -offering- in the past? Have you rented or considered renting retail premises? Are there any other sales opportunities that you have considered or are considering? What interests you about this particular opportunity?	0–5 desire for a long-term space **3**	Target: 4/5 are 4+
Section B: 10.15–10.30 Are the existing solutions good enough to solve their problem/meet their needs or desires?	That the existing ways to sell could be improved upon	Thinking about where you can sell today (a) What appeals about each opportunity? (b) Is there anything that concerns you? (c) Describe your ideal trading opportunity...	YES or NO to a new way to sell **YES**	Target: 3/5 YES
Section C: 10.30–10.40 Are they prepared to take the necessary actions to get another solution?	1) Prepared to invest time & money into a new sales opportunity 2) Prepared for continual changing environment, trial & error	1) Can you give me any examples of where you invested time and money to make some sales? Do you have an example of when you were one of the first to try out a new sales opportunity? 2) Given what you know about this potential opportunity, are you prepared to invest time and a little money to get yourself set up as a trader? How do you feel about working within this new project where there is going to be a period of trial and error for everyone?	1) YES or NO prepared **YES** 2) YES or NO prepared **NO**	Target: 1) 3/5 YES Target: 2) 3/5 YES
Section D: (Optional) 10.40–10.55 How do they feel about your idea? 10.55–11 Close	1) Shop units are appealing 2) Terms, conditions & costs are acceptable	1) Let's go into the market and look at the empty shop units. (a) Are there particular shop unit(s) that appeal to you? (b) Do you have any questions? (c) Do you have any suggestions? 2) Take a look at this draft paperwork (a) Is there anything that you are pleased to see? (b) Do you have any concerns or questions? (c) Are there any changes you would propose?	1) 0–5 interest in a shop unit **4** 2) YES, NO or MAYBE will agree **MAYBE**	Target: 1) 3/5 are 3+ Target: 2) 3/5 YES or MAYBE

Remember that you need to take fresh CHECKLISTS and CORE paperwork into each interview as you need to fill out specific information for each individual.

Try it for yourself!

Remember that you can download the templates at productdoctor.co.uk

TOP TIPS

Audio record the interview so you can concentrate on what they are telling you rather than on making notes

Remember to probe for more information using 'The Trilogy' set of questions to help you

Take a fresh copy of the full research script into every interview to log individual's details and keep consistency

COMMON PITFALLS

If you are talking more than 20 per cent of the time then you are selling, not listening!

Influencing the interviewees during the interview to answer questions in a particular way

Busting your interview time as you are talking hypothetically and not shutting down irrelevance

STEP 7

ANALYSE & DECIDE

With all the interviews in one group complete, it is time to analyse the interviews and see what evidence you now have. The challenge is to be as objective as you can. You will be able to add together all the individual scores against the measures you decided on in Step 5 (Measures and targets) and see your overall scores for the group. You will also have plenty of additional insight that will help you to refine all elements of your hypothesis and your target audiences, and further detail the proposition. With all this information you will be able to make a decision about what to do next. The ultimate decision is whether to stop or pursue. The evidence you now have may show you that your assumptions were wrong and it is time to divert your efforts elsewhere. Or you may decide to pursue, going down one of two different paths: You may need to gather more evidence, or you may now have enough confidence to proceed into delivery.

Listen back to your interviews

The purpose of listening back to the audio recording is to help you be objective and try to hear what the interviewee said rather than what you think that they said. It will also help you to remember the earlier interviews, as the last interview will be the dominant one in your memory. Try to listen out for the negative and constructive rather than just the positive! The scoring will help you do this as I often find I heard something more loudly than the reality. Perhaps one or two people said it, but in my head, I thought it was far more. Perhaps it was something that I wanted to hear. I always learn something from research conversations that I did not expect, so sometimes those points ring more loudly in my head as they were surprises. Just be careful as our minds can play funny tricks on us.

If you used the CORE and CHECKLISTS templates for each of the interviews, then go get them so that you can have each one in front of you as you listen back to the audio. They will help jog your memory as you will see any notes you made (you may have time stamped some) and the scores that you assigned against targets during the interview.

Go somewhere quiet. Hover your finger above the pause and rewind buttons and prick your ears up. You will find yourself pausing while you write down what you just heard and rewinding to check you heard it correctly.

Calculate scores and gather important additional insights

Compare group scores against your group targets

In Step 6 (Conduct interviews) at the end of the interview, while you still have the interviewee with you, you should have assigned an individual score for each interviewee against each target that you are measuring. You will have another opportunity to check that score while you are listening back to the recordings.

Now you can look back at all the individual scores and see how they measure against the group targets you set in Step 5 (Measures and targets). You will then be able to see if you hit the targets and whether the evidence validates your assumptions or not.

Keep the scoring very simple:

- Let's say you used a scale to score a particular measure from 0–5 and the group target was 4/5 are a 4+ (four out of five scored four or more). Out of the five interviewees in this group, 3/5 scored a 4 or more (three out of five scored a four or more). Then the group score is 3/5 (three out of five) and that is a 'fail'.
- If another group target was measured as a YES or NO and the group target was 3/5 (three out of five) say YES. Out of the five interviewees in this group, 4/5 said YES (four out of the five said YES). Then the group score is 4/5 (four out of five) and that is a 'pass'.

Remember that if you have different group profiles, you will need to keep the calculations for each of the sets of interviews separate. (This is easy if you are using the templates, as you will have different group profiles on their own sets of templates.)

At this point you may feel a bit frustrated as perhaps you have failed on some of the measures, yet you know exactly what to do to improve the scores. It is likely that through the interviews, you learned what needs changing in the proposition. Perhaps that is about the customer and/or user profile whose problems, need or desires you are addressing. Maybe it is about the problem, need or desire itself, or about the benefits that they are seeking from a solution. Or maybe it's about the current solutions on offer. Hang on to this information as we go through what to do with additional insight and how to show this in the decision that you make later on in this step.

Additional insights

In addition to working out the group score, there is going to be lots of other information that will help you improve your idea further. You may have hours of interviews to listen back to. Some people find it useful to write down some themes and important insights after each interview, before they listen back to the audio. You can then use this as a starting list for when you listen back to the audio and write up your notes into a report.

To help you get a view across all the interviews, you may find it useful to develop some generic questions to answer and as you listen back, make notes against each. You can also record numbers to help you see how consistent certain views were. Again, this will help keep you neutral.

Here is an example set of generic questions you can pick from to help you spot these additional insights:

- Where did people agree?
- Where did they differ?
- What had a big impact?
- What were they surprised by?
- What did they find interesting?
- What were they indifferent to?
- What did they like?

- What did they hate?
- What were their biggest concerns?
- What issue did they keep returning to?
- What suggestions did they make?
- What did they want us to change?
- What did they misunderstand?
- What criticisms did they make?

Listen out for where interviewees misunderstand something you say to them. When we are carrying out the actual interviews, we are trying to make sure that the interviewee understands what we are saying and asking them. That is our focus. But when we listen back, it is an opportunity to then note what we had to explain again. This is very important information as an indication of where we need to be clearer when explaining a new proposition going forward.

Again, in the interview you may skim over negative insight or criticism. For example, maybe the interviewee does not really fit your target segment, but you carried on the interview as you had them there in front of you. The danger is that you are gathering insight and counting targets from someone who does not match your segments. Or perhaps they criticised an idea that you put to them, and you can hear yourself persuading them that they are wrong, that this is in fact a great idea! Now is the chance to catch yourself doing this and correct it before you count a positive score against a target when you should not.

Deciding to PURSUE

You can decide to pursue even if you failed the test

You may not have hit the scores that you set in Step 5 (Measures and targets) but you may have a feeling from the group that you interviewed that you can appeal to a different target group or that the scores would improve if you changed something in the value proposition. Maybe the wrong measures were used but you had good insight to support the customer and/or user problem, need and/or desire. Maybe it triggered a whole new idea!

Think carefully about the responses from different interviewees if you had a mix of ages or other factors. You may find that you are hitting the mark with some but not other people in the group. You might have a hunch that there might be a pattern that you want to explore further. Perhaps the variable that you used to create the mix becomes a recruitment criterion to add to the group profile in another round of interviews. For example, you recruited a mix of ages but found that your hypothesis resonated more with the 35 to 50 year olds, so you now add that age bracket into your demographic recruitment criteria and carry out another round of interviews to see if you are right.

You now have valuable evidence of a hypothesis that does not pass the test so you can use those insights to make changes. Often called a 'pivot', you may want to make changes and keep going with a different version of this idea. In these cases, you need to take what you know and go back to Step 1 (Write hypothesis). While there are no shortcuts, it may be that you just need to make some tweaks.

Pursue and move onto the next set of risky assumptions

You may still have further risky assumptions or different value propositions and target groups to address before you can say that you do indeed have a really good idea. You may have started out with a number of different elements to test and found that it was too big for one set of interviews, so you need to take them back through the seven steps. (Once you have carried out this process a few times you will be able to whizz through them.)

Maybe you started with just one of the customer and/or user segments you identified and you need to go to the others now. In the indoor market project example, the potential test traders were not the only group, there were also risky assumptions around the market visitors; the punters who needed to spend money with the traders.

Maybe through your initial research you have uncovered another important segment, or perhaps you want to try out a refinement to your target customer and/or user profiles.

Maybe you have found needs and benefits that you think could be more crucial than the ones you started out with. How about if a bigger problem exists than the one you identified?

Again, please take all new thoughts back through Step 1 (Write hypothesis), even if it is a box-ticking exercise and you do not actually need to make any changes until you get to Step 3 (Create questions).

Summarising your decision

The decision that you make will need some further clarification beyond just a PURSUE or STOP. The clarification needs to take into account not just the scores for the group and whether you passed the target for each measure that validates your initial assumptions, but also what your next step is going to be. Here is a way to consider how to summarise your decision:

- Whether you are going to PURSUE and move forward, PURSUE and run some more tests or STOP.
- Whether you passed or failed all the measures in The Really Good Idea Test. (Remember that you can still pursue even if you failed.)
- What your next steps are going to be.

Guidance for pursuers!

If you have more to test you can skim but not skip steps. Even though you are now familiar with the seven steps in The Really Good Idea Test, if you have decided to pursue your idea, you must go back to Step 1 (Write hypothesis) and work through them chronologically. At the minimum, skim read each step, paying particular attention to the common pitfalls to avoid so that you do not fall into those traps that will reduce the value of the overall test.

For example, maybe you started with a small number of interviewees from the target customer and/or user group and you feel you need to increase the sample to give yourself more confidence. If you started with five interviewees, and you have a mass market proposition, you may decide that you need to hear from more.

If you are not changing anything at all and are just repeating the test with more of the same, then you are good to go. Use the same research script you created (CORE + CHECKLISTS) and carry on. It is very important that you keep the same questions and measures, so as you do more groups you can genuinely add up the answers from all groups. For the same reason, if you find you need to ask for additional information, then add new questions rather than replacing the old ones. This consistency in questions is really important, particularly if there are long periods between doing the work and/or different interviewers are involved.

If you are making any changes at all, I urge you to please go back to Step 1 (Write hypothesis) and check that what you have written for the previous round is applicable to this round. Then move chronologically through the steps so that you do not miss anything important in the way that you create the CORE (Steps 1 to 5), your CHECKLISTS (Step 6) and capture RESULTS (Step 7).

Don't get stuck in a continual testing loop! There is no question about it. You will never be able to address all risks to a level where you are totally comfortable. You are an innovator, so by your nature, it means that you are the type of person who is more prepared to take risks than others. The Really Good Idea Test gives you a way to reduce the level of the risks and by doing so, to turn them into calculated risks. The important point is that you have recognised fundamental risks and have attempted to do something about them before investing too heavily on building solutions. You can only do so much without getting stuck in a continual testing loop where you are constantly questioning, so you need to accept that and move on!

Be honest with yourself – run more tests if you need to. So here is the opposite scenario: You are so excited that you have passed The Really Good Idea Test that you raid the bank account and plough straight into building solutions. So just take a step back and question:

- Have you interviewed enough people?
- Have you addressed all the riskiest assumptions you had in Step 2 (Identify risks) as perhaps there were too many for one test?
- Have you addressed the most important target groups of people from Step 1 (Write hypothesis) 'people map', value propositions

work and Step 4 (Find interviewees)? Perhaps you have a few different segments of customer groups? Or perhaps for example, you have interviewed users but not the paying customers? Or perhaps you have some important influencers where some risky assumptions lurk?

Deciding to STOP

This has not been wasted work! While you may have failed The Really Good Idea Test, all is good!

You have gathered some really valid evidence to add to your bank of knowledge. Remember back in Step 2 (Identify risks) where we look for evidence to support our theories? Well this is now part of that. It has now become part of the reason why you are going, or not going in a particular direction and why you are therefore making certain decisions. If you are working in an organisation, it is really valuable information to share with others so you can all learn. You may be sparking ideas for something else.

What is more, you have NOT wasted effort and/or money building a product or service that does not have a market! You are now free to go and spend your efforts wisely elsewhere. Maybe you can start over again with your next really good idea?

Use this opportunity to review your own research skills

Listening back to the audio, you will be able to review how well you performed as a researcher. Go back to the Step 6 (Conduct interviews) exercise where you got to practice your research skills and score yourself. There will always be room for you to improve. Even the most experienced researchers can slip into bad habits. Listen out in particular for whether you talked too much or led the interviewee. Did you pick up all the clues that they gave you and did you allow any hypotheticals to creep in?

Completing The Really Good Idea Test templates

- -

Are you working on your own idea as you go through this book?
    If so, then there are two templates to work on.

1. Complete the group scores into the CORE document

Add the group score to all the CORE documents in the group.
    With the group scores updated next to the group targets that you
set in Step 5 (Measures & targets), these are now documents that
have all the information you need to explain the decision you are
going to make and how you got there. They are useful for your own
future reference as well as if you need to communicate with others.
    Here is the indoor market project updated CORE template. It
shows that the group scores for this group profile have been added.
You can also see the original individual measures e.g. '0–5 desire
for a long-term space' and the Target e.g. '4/5 are 4+' that you
established in Step 5 (Measures and targets). To recap you are just
adding the group score in the final column.

MEASURES & TARGETS ⑤	
0-5 desire for a long-term space	Target: 4/5 are 4+ **Group Score: 4/5. Pass**
YES or NO to a new way to sell	Target: 3/5 YES **Group Score: 4/5. Pass**
1) YES or NO prepared	Target: 1) 3/5 YES **Group Score: 3/5. Pass**
2) YES or NO prepared	Target: 2) 3/5 YES **Group Score: 3/5. Pass**
1) 0-5 interest in a shop unit	Target: 1) 3/5 are 3+ **Group Score: 2/5. Fail**
2) YES, NO or MAYBE with feasible changes	Target: 2) 3/5 YES or MAYBE **Group Score: 2/5. Fail**

2. Produce the RESULTS

Now you can move on to the use the final template – RESULTS. This template works as a summary for each group of interviews with spaces to share your decision, rationale and additional insights.

The RESULTS one page provides a succinct format to see the overall findings across the group of interviews that have been conducted. If you need more detail, then you can of course refer back to your CORE and CHECKLISTS templates so these become supporting documents.

Here is the RESULTS template, where you can record your Decision and Additional Insights.

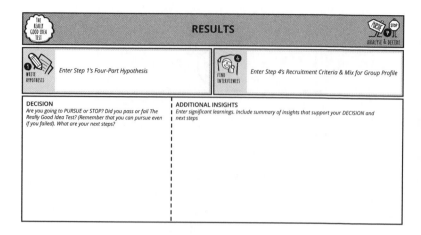

What do I write in these boxes?

1. Copy over Step 1 (Write hypothesis) and Step 4 (Group profile) from the CORE template. The information is repeated here for two reasons: Firstly, in case this one page is separated from the completed CORE documents you will still be able to reference what it is about and secondly, as you may want to use it as a standalone document to communicate just the results.

2. DECISION

Here you can record your Decision and you can see the prompts to include whether you are going to PURSUE or STOP, whether this particular group passed or failed The Really Good Idea Test and your next steps.

3. ADDITIONAL INSIGHTS

There is also a box to record your Additional Insights, which are significant pieces of information you have discovered that often help to improve upon your idea, further support your decision or important points to note as you move forward.

Here is a completed RESULTS document for the indoor market project with the potential test traders group:

RESULTS

THE REALLY GOOD IDEA TEST

① WRITE HYPOTHESIS

Our hypothesis is that we can generate full-price rentals in 6 months from all 20 empty shops if the right mix of traders are given free test trading opportunities within a broader programme of activity

④ FIND INTERVIEWEES

Group Profile: 5 Potential Test Traders
- *Eligible to trade in the UK*
- *Old enough to sign up to a contract*
- *Have a current offering suitable for a shop unit*
- *Interested in a full-time retail opportunity*
- *Mix: Age, gender, retail offering*

DECISION: PURSUE!

Test failed on points that can be addressed to turn the scores positive.

Desire is big enough and the solution is attractive. Although some had no experience of similar environment, it did not unnerve them.

1). Make change to trading hours in clause 8 to turn Traders' scores positive

2). Make assurances around habitable state of shop units

3). Next week, run The Really Good Idea Test with 5 potential local punters to address risky assumptions around frequency & spend

4). If positive, proceed with launch plan

ADDITIONAL INSIGHTS:

It is normal & expected by traders that they will need to take risks on new sales opportunities & invest some of their own funds

Reassurance by market management team needed regarding the condition of shop units at time committing to the test trade

Some traders will be very involved with marketing & have existing online followers, experience & to generate footfall

Some traders will want to share shop units ...

Check on 'shop use' rules with the council

Traders know other potential traders so are an important channel to spread the word

Collaborate with local farmers market to share footfall?

Opportunities could be more attractive if hours were extended to Sundays and for restaurants, fu into the evening

In this example you can see that while the Decision is to PURSUE, the test failed on addressable points, which are around the specific terms and conditions of the trading hours in the contract and the habitable state of shop units. When you look back at the CORE document, you will see these failures were both in section D, so this is a useful back-up document in case you are asked for further information. You also have the CORE and CHECKLISTS with your handwritten scores and notes that you used in each individual interview if you need to refer further back.

You can also see that the decision to PURSUE in this case is to go to another group profile and see how their risky assumptions fare. This will require going back to Step 1 (Write hypothesis) to make any appropriate changes and then finding risky assumptions in Step 2 (Identify risks). It is possible to move very quickly and feasible that the interviews could be carried out within the week. After all, the potential market punters should be easy to find, shopping and drinking in the coffee shops that surround the indoor market area.

The Additional Insights support both the Decision and next steps as well as giving some useful insights to help the broader programme to move forward

Try it for yourself!

- -

Remember that you can also download these templates from productdoctor.co.uk.

TOP TIPS

Stay objective as you listen back to the research interviews (see guidance)

Use the RESULTS template to easily share your decision and the rationale behind it

Use this step to review your research skills and see where you can improve

COMMON PITFALLS

Hearing what you want to hear from the interviews

Getting stuck in a continual testing loop

Moving on to build or delivery when there are still high-risk assumptions that need testing

MOVING FORWARD

I wrote *The Really Good Idea Test* as a simple do-it-yourself way for people with new ideas to see if they have hit on something interesting. For those innovators who want to forge forward with gusto, it is intended as an anti-waste exercise, asking them to take a moment to focus on the value that they think they can create before they start investing too heavily. For those people who have an idea buzzing around their head but never seem to do anything with it, it can give some simple steps to get off the starting block. For anyone who wants to have more confidence in their ideas, this test will help you get evidence that boosts your confidence to pursue, or give you evidence to stop.

The approach can be used to examine ideas in a different way so that all the great ideas have a chance to see the light of day rather than being forgotten or never pursued.

If you have passed The Really Good Idea Test, then you can be more confident in moving forward, working to make your new features, products, services and projects a reality. This is where many other processes, best practice guidance and books kick in. They can help you with user-centred design, how to create early mock-ups for feedback and how to take an iterative design approach as you create prototypes and early versions of the product. There are some really good approaches that you have been practising in this test, and they will help you to continue to avoid some common pitfalls as you move forward.

If the test has helped you to make a decision to stop on this occasion, I want to congratulate you and welcome you to the exclusive Product Killers Club! Let's celebrate the time you have just freed up to put into something that has a better chance of success. The great news is that you now know where to come to test your next idea (and I am sure that there will be many more). You may even have got a whole new idea out of killing the old one!

Good practice to continue as you move forward

Keep people at the heart of innovation

During this test you cannot have avoided being totally focused on people. Your customers and/or users, stakeholders and influencers have all had a look in! If you want to continue to give your idea as good a chance of success as you can, then keep these people at the front and centre of all that you do. Continue to see all your ideas from their point of view, pose questions while standing in their shoes and know that your ideas will live or die by their hand. Stay true to their problems, needs and desires.

Create personas to represent your group profiles

Once you have built confidence in your group profile description, you use a 'persona' to represent it. You are likely to end up with a number of personas to represent each of the different group profiles you have. (I would resist from having more than around five as you don't want to make life too confusing!)

The persona is usually made up of a picture with annotated description that put them into that group profile. So, for example, Matilda is the person who represents your largest customer segment. Here is a photo of her, along with a description of her daily life. You can see her attitudes to 'x' and her feelings about 'y'. You can search online for examples of how to present these personas.

It is great to be able to show personas to others as it brings your target groups to life – they become more real. You can keep these up to date as you continue to engage with different customers and users and learn more about them. The visual personas work really well when colleagues and collaborators can see them. It is a constant reminder to keep these people at the heart of what you do. You must continue to question 'What would <Matilda> think of this?'

Keep your hypothesis up to date

One common pitfall is that innovators start building something, spend lots of money, forget to keep checking what is happening in the outside world and when they eventually launch the world has moved on and the solution is no longer required/needed or the desire has been satisfied by an alternative means.

As you move forward, make sure that you keep checking your hypothesis and that the four elements are still current.

Being able to also refer to an up-to-date hypothesis at any time is very useful for collaborators and colleagues who are helping you deliver your idea. They will see what you are trying to achieve, who you are intending to create benefit for and what you need them to do to fulfil your goals. People (stakeholders, team members, partners and suppliers) will be able to support you much more effectively when they understand the bigger picture of where you are coming from and who the beneficiaries are.

Work incrementally so you can easily iterate

To continue this anti-waste approach and to create an environment where you can continually be testing and improving, try to work incrementally. That means in practice, that you split the work up into bite-sized chunks and only spend money on each bit at a time, checking as you go. It enables you to test things out with customers and/or users as you develop them and if you need to go back and make changes, there is less waste.

Continue to use this test every time you have an idea

You are going to continue to have all sorts of ideas as you move forward and in every case, you can turn them into a hypothesis starting with Step 1 (Write hypothesis). Each idea you test is likely to be more detailed than the last but nonetheless, it is an idea and you need to start by making sure it is a good one!

No matter how big or small, if you are unsure about what to do and if you are questioning whether to spend time, energy and money, you can use The Really Good Idea Test.

Imagine that you have an idea about what programming language to use to code up your new online service, or you are wondering which partners you should work with, or whether you should go through a particular sales channel, or employ a particular customer payment method, or which feature to next build, or a new market to address, or which customer problem you should fix first and so on. In each of these cases, you will need to work out what your customer and/or user benefit is right at the start in Step 1 (Write hypothesis). If you do not get this right, you are at risk of developing solutions that do not meet their needs.

Take the example of what programming language your developers should use. Of course, you would need to look at how the end user is experiencing the product to see if it makes any difference to them; but how about whoever needs to analyse product performance and understand customer behaviour in your team? I am sure that they (perhaps it is you) will have something to say. They would be an internal user of the data, so identifying them up front and writing a value proposition for them will put you on the right path to delivering a solution that meets their needs as well as the end customer.

Moving forward in different environments

You are still not at the point of doing a business case!

In the first chapter of this book, we talked about how to get your company, colleagues and/or investors on board with The Really Good Idea Test. This included how to ask for access to a very small budget to carry out some really early idea testing all by yourself. We ran through the explanations you can give around it being too early for you to produce a useful business case and, guess what, . . . it probably still is too early! Right now, if you have passed the test, you have a bank of evidence that shows your initial idea is now something that looks like a pretty good idea. The chances are that you still do not know enough about the solution to create a meaningful business case, but you are now ready to spend a bit more to get you closer.

How to share your test results

If you have decided to pursue your idea and you need to pitch for some resources to move forward, (perhaps you have a potential investor, partner, manager or company stage gate to pass), you should now feel confident to present it. If you use the templates, it will be easier to tell the story.

You can share your RESULTS document as it recaps on your hypothesis, the group that you have tested your idea with, the rationale for your decision to pursue and the additional insights that you have. The CORE and CHECKLISTS are a good accompaniment as they show how you got to this point.

With the templates in play, you have a very logical way to tell your story structured around the seven steps of the test. It is good to start with the decision and next steps and then go back to Step 1 (Write hypothesis) and talk through what you did. If you did circle around the test a few times, then it is good to explain what you learned from each group and how you iterated to move onto the next. You can also share the seven steps diagram that you will find at the start of this book. Below is an example of how you can structure the conversation. You will see that I suggest you 'Point to' in some places. This refers to where you can point to sections of your templates. You will also see where you can add the specific details of your really good idea. I have put those in < > brackets.

Here is a structure you can use for sharing your results:

I am here to present an idea that we want to pursue. It has been through The Really Good Idea Test which means that we have enough evidence to show that it does look like it is a good idea.

(Point to RESULTS) We tested out our hypothesis with <x> group(s) of target customers <and users> and we have proof that their <problems, needs and/or desires> exist, that current solutions are not meeting their needs well enough <or that there is no current solution> and that their <problem, need and/or desire> is big enough for them to take the actions we need them to for us to realise our goals.

We found out that (Point to Additional Insights on RESULTS) . . . . So we have made those changes to . . . we circled back around the test a few times . . . and are now ready to take our next steps which are . . .

Here is how we got to this point:

(Point to Step 1 box on CORE) First, we spent time writing our hypothesis, to be clear about our overall goal and idea and who we could add value for <read out your hypothesis>.

(Point to Step 2 box on CORE) Then, we identified where our biggest, riskiest assumptions were. We carried out some desk research and found some evidence to support some of these, but we still wanted more as they are fundamental to the success of the overall idea.

(Point to Step 3 box on CORE) So we crafted interview questions which we put to a group of profiled customers (and users) in structured face-to-face interviews. (Point to Step 4 on CORE).

(Point to interview sections A to D column on CORE) Our biggest concerns were about whether <the problem, need or desire exists, whether there was any room for a new solution or whether existing solutions were good enough and whether the group(s) were prepared to take the necessary actions to get a new solution. Finally, as we had already thought about our solution and we were in front of some of our target audience, we took the opportunity to get some feedback>.

*(Point to Step 5 on CORE) We set up **targets and measures** for the responses so we could see whether as a group, we were able to validate and reduce those risky assumptions or not. These scores plus the additional insights that we got have led us to this point.*

*(Go back to **RESULTS** and reiterate what you are suggesting the next step is and what you need to achieve it.)*

Invest incrementally

When we talk of 'investment', we are not just talking about hard cash injection. There are other types of resources that you may need to help you progress your idea other than money, like land, materials and labour. Maybe you feel that this doesn't apply to you as perhaps you just need to rely on your own time to move forward and you have accounted for that.

Whatever your position, the chances are that you do need some resources of some description. Maybe you already have some funds that are waiting to be spent. Maybe you are working in an organisation where the funding is set up to be awarded in small chunks as a way to limit financial exposure. Perhaps that is linked to some kind of pre-defined stage-based process where you need to demonstrate your progress against certain criteria. If you can pass those criteria, then you are able to access more investment to move into the next stage.

If you need to make the case for resource investment from someone else, it is a good idea to ask for incremental investment. The chances are that you have an idea of what you now want to build but you may not have a functioning prototype or have had any detailed customer and/or user input to that yet. So, the support you need is just enough to get you through this next period of early product, service, experience or solution design where you can engage customers and/or users to make sure you are staying true to what they want and need. Then you will be back for more!

Investing incrementally and stopping to make decisions at regular intervals will help you to move bit by bit, stopping you from jumping ahead too far. It will encourage you to keep checking what you are doing against your customer and/or user needs and make sure that you continue to build to their needs and desires. This positioning works well for those who are awarding funding and/or resources as it is a prudent approach. It is, of course, a good idea to adopt this approach even if you already have access to the funds.

Working with naysayers

It is a common scene and one I have experienced many times. In fact, it is inevitable. You are presenting your results and your case for next-stage funding and there it is, the cries of 'Why don't you . . . ?' 'Have you thought about. . . ?' 'I think that you should . . . '. By now, I hope that these objector/proposers have listened to your RESULTS. If you talked through the RESULTS in the way that I suggest, they will know that there is a seven-step process to evaluate each of these suggestions.

So if you get a suggestion you can work it through with the group or the objector/proposer, starting from Step 1 to turn it into a testable hypothesis.

Here is a structure for a conversation with a naysayer:

Start by asking them what their overall goal is to make sure that you are all coming from the same place. For example, is it to generate more money per customer or to create a stickier experience and increase customer loyalty, or is it to create a better user experience in the hope of improving satisfaction scores? You may find that the 'objector/proposer' has a different overall goal in mind, in which case a priority call will need to be made.

*Help them to articulate what the idea is and to do that succinctly.
You may find that this is a really big and useful thought and you
want to go gather more evidence or you may find that it is a detail
that you are not yet ready for, for example a technology to use for
building the solution.*

*Discuss who you are creating value for. So, for example, if they are
suggesting a different segment, work through constructing the whole
value proposition statement so you can clearly see what they assume
to be the problems, needs and desires and how they think they can
add benefit above and beyond what exists today.*

*Lastly, talk through with them what action you need people to take
so that you can realise the goal.*

Once you have been through this further definition, if their suggestion still seems like a good idea, you can explain that the next thing
to do is Step 2 (Identify risks), where you will analyse where evidence
exists for high-impacting elements and where it does not. Evidence
is the key. If it does not exist to sufficient levels, then we need to continue with the test and see whether to stop or pursue it further.

If you have some kind of management or investor board or group
to satisfy, then you can see that you now have a structure to help
them evaluate all new ideas. You have a test to work out whether
those ideas are good or not. If you can get the group/board into this
way of thinking, you will make it much easier for them to be able to
assess whether an idea is good and also easier for other innovators to
propose only good ideas.

The Really Good Idea Test's seven steps have been tried and tested far and wide

The Really Good Idea Test has been developed through many years
of working with new ideas; from start-up concepts to big corporate
product ideas, from community-based projects to those with high
international revenue streams and with senior execs who have lots
of business experience to people with none.

I know that these steps and tools work across the board, cross sector and cross industry. So this is a big thanks to all of you who have shared their ideas with me over the years as colleagues, collaborators, clients, friends, participants in my workshops and 'patients' in my 'Product Doctor Surgeries'. Without all of you, I would not be able to make such a bold statement!

I would like to thank John Spindler, Oli Pinch, Mike Butcher, Ian Merricks, James Cooper, Alastair Moore and Daniel Appelquist for enabling me to engage with hundreds of participants through my workshops and Product Doctor Surgeries spanning a massive range of sectors including Energy, Fashion, Health, Retail, Digital Media, Food, Mass Media, Automotive, Sport, Education, Finance, Hospitality, Gaming, Technology and Mobile Applications, Music and Travel.

I would also like to thank colleagues and clients in particular sectors where I have further developed and proved my approaches working on qualitative research projects, leading training workshops and coaching sessions: Celia Francis, Lauren Bigelow and Melissa Lang (Digital and Media), Bill Best, Katrina Damianou, Horace Ho and Tony Kypreos (Mobile, Networking and Applications), Chris Norris and Dougald Hine (Local Council and Community), Colin Hayhurst and Sean Ryan (Science and Research), Marc Abraham and Anne Fairbrother (Retail and Finance), Anna Gudmundson (Health and Fitness), Liz Tyler, Zoe Botterill, Caroline Wheeler, Tendayi Viki, Craig Strong and Richard Stagg (Education and Publishing).

The Really Good Idea Test principles were used to create this book

Big chunks of this test have been tested, validated and improved upon as I have delivered real workshops, coaching sessions and drop in surgeries across all those sectors and industries. While testing them out was not the main objective (clients – calm down!) this has happened organically as I continually improve and iterate based on feedback. Creating a hypothesis in four parts, doing a 'people map', The Trilogy questions, the exercise to practice research skills, the checklists for introducing and closing interviews, the tables and the four-section structure for interviews are just a few examples of those chunks.

As I started to write this book, I realised that there would be great value in getting feedback from potential readers. I was determined to work on chapters one by one so that I could incrementally integrate their feedback in short bursts to iterate and improve as I go. At this point I want to thank those who have helped me with this process: First off, the Pearson team – the visionary Richard Stagg for his encouragement and support, Eloise Cook, Lou Attwood, Dr. Priyadharshini Dhanagopal and Amer Parikh. Next to thank is Nic Hinton for the graphics and my marvellous reader-reviewers, starting with my reviewer-in-chief Stuart Revell, then the wonderful Tom Hume, Laura Thomas, Dave Sarson, Allison Strachan, Gerald Shalet, Helen Shalet and Julie Harris who gave feedback to each chapter as this book was written.

How using The Really Good Idea Test helped me to position this book

I wanted to test out my hypothesis that this book was going to have a diverse set of readers. So I started talking with all sorts of people: From students to professors, hairdressers to builders, corporate to council employees, serial innovators to product managers, CEOs to sole operators and more. All of them had this one thing in common – they had a new idea. This helped to set the tone of this book, that The Really Good Idea Test should speak to everyone, those with experience working on new ideas and those without, those who are working alone or with teams, those working in a larger organisation or totally independently.

I needed some help with the book title. I already had a list of possible titles and the publishers had given me a strong steer: What would people search for? Of course I had to get out there and see what I could learn by asking potential readers. By doing this I found out that there are people who buy this sort of book to read themselves and people who will buy this book as a gift for someone else. So I have both customers (those who buy the book) and users (those who read the book). They may or may not be the same person. This sounds quite obvious now I say it, but that had not really struck me before. Of course when you are so close to something you don't see the obvious and it takes potential customers and/or users to tell you!

Through exploring many different options with these potential customers and users, the resounding advice they gave me was that the best title would be to 'say it as it is'. This is what they would search for online and what would grab their attention. I pondered on this and thought back over the years. I have listened very carefully to people talk about their ideas. They most often start by saying, with some excitement, 'I've got this really good idea. . . '. So there it was: *The Really Good Idea Test*. This title got a positive response from potential customers and users. They certainly knew what the book was about with no further explanation.

A quizzical smile seems to break across people's faces when I tell them the title. When I have asked them what they were thinking, they explained that they were playing around with the title:

That it is a test to see if you have a really good idea

That the idea test is, in itself, really good

That it is a really good idea to take the test if you have an idea

I hope that these resonate with you and thank you for reading this book. You can find me at productdoctor.co.uk.

TOP TIPS

Keep all your completed templates as they are an important bank of evidence you can refer back to

Continue to keep customers and users at the heart of everything that you do

Use the seven-step approach in this test as a way to handle feedback, new ideas and objections

COMMON PITFALLS

Picking the right point in time to move forward to develop a business case and/or develop your solution

Resourcing the development, delivery and launch of the whole idea rather than managing it incrementally

Letting an idea roll around and around in your head when you can now so easily put it to The Really Good Idea Test and see if you should pursue it or not!

Index

___